Ruthfulness

EDUCATE · ADVOCATE · ACCESS

A mother's journey to accepting autism

RUTH BRUNSON

Published by Richter Publishing LLC
www.richterpublishing.com

Book Cover Design: Richter Publishing LLC

Editors: Margarita Martinez & Marisa Beetz

Book Formatting: Monica San Nicolas

ISBN-13: 978-1-945812-74-3 paperback

DISCLAIMER

DEDICATION

To my son, thank you for making me Ruthfulness.
You have made me full of life and purpose—you were
my missing piece.

CONTENTS

ACKNOWLEDGMENTS

Thank you to my husband, who encouraged me to write not only my blog but also this book. Without his example and initial push, I would not have started, let alone finished, this project.

Thank you to all of my friends who taught me about autism before autism was important or relevant to me. Those moments were funny but serious and are marked in my heart forever.

Thank you to those who follow and read my blog, as well as stay connected via social media.

Also, to all of the parents of children with autism and developmental delays—this book is for you. The system of early intervention is in need of improvement and reform. Our children need more advocates and access to the right education and therapy. You are not alone.

FOREWORD

My dear friend Ruth Brunson and I met on our first move-in day at the University of South Florida (USF) in 2002. It was a meeting racked with random adventure. I had a film crew following me around to do a piece for the local news on new college students and the rising costs of schooling. My parents and I agreed to this encounter on a whim and upon seeing the camera crew, microphones, large cameras, and equipment, I swiftly attempted to back out several times. Despite my efforts, they stuck with us. Upon entering our new campus apartment, I was nervous, overwhelmed, and worried about how my new roommates would perceive this intrusion.

However, I was greeted without judgment as Ruth welcomed me (and the crew) into our new home. My new roommate didn't bat an eye as she engaged them in conversation, and they even helped her set up her bed! That one moment that had started off as overwhelming, nerve-racking, and potentially embarrassing turned into a lifetime friendship that I am forever grateful for. We experienced all of the challenges that life brings you. Ruth and I lived together through several apartments, additional roommates, boyfriends, and new jobs. We participated in each other's weddings and welcomed new babies!

New babies brought new challenges that we would have never dreamed of.

When Ruth shared that her son could be diagnosed with autism, I knew the challenges and heartache she could potentially face. I also knew of her strength, passion, determination, and will to succeed, along with her steadfast commitment to her family that would guide her in the face of this new life path. Conversations with Ruth circled around the diagnosis controversy, differences in family opinions, challenges with marriage, immense struggles and triumphs with therapies, and the discrimination and ill will toward her son from teachers—and through all of this, I knew she would be okay.

Ruth would not only be okay on this journey, but I knew that she would persevere, she would exceed expectations, she would fight and advocate for her son, as well as for her family. She would come out on the other side even more educated than before, a model for other parents and a comfort to others just starting this journey—far down the path or somewhere in between. With her background in teaching and her experience with the school districts and IEPs, along with being a parent, wife, sister, and daughter, she is one of the best people to share her journey of love, acceptance, determination, empowerment, resilience, and strength.

Two years after meeting Ruth that unexpected day

at USF, I began my career supporting families with children with autism. She witnessed my journey and growth as I learned a new job, received training, and experienced interactions with new students with autism and their families. Ruth sat night after night at the kitchen table listening to stories of the school day, laughing with me, and lending a shoulder to cry on when my emotions of the day got the best of me. I could always count on her to listen, care, and provide unconditional love to me as a friend. I know that her story and her message should be received in that same way.

As a board-certified behavior analyst, I am also a certified infant toddler developmental specialist, certified RDI program consultant, and have been working to support families with children with autism and varying abilities since 2004. I have been in the field of child development since 2000 and have a bachelor's degree in psychology and master's degree in applied behavior analysis. I have grown through this field with Ruth at my side as a close friend supporting me along this journey. Since moving to California six years ago, I regret that I could not be there physically to support Ruth on her path as she did for me. However, I am confident that Ruth and her story will be the guiding light for so many parents, family members, and professionals as they embark upon the adventure of autism.

Ruth's story and mission to share her knowledge and

hope with others is so valuable and relevant today and will continue to grow in its importance as the rate of autism climbs and continues to increase.

With the autism rate at 1 in 68 children (according to the CDC), the value of this book is immeasurable.

Ruth's story will provide value to parents who worry and need guidance, professionals who will benefit from the perspective of a teacher and parent, and anyone looking to learn and grow from another person's experience and journey through advocating for their special needs child.

Kathryn M. Bovino, M.A., BCBA

INTRODUCTION

The first time I met my best friend was in August 2002 when I transferred from Keuka College in New York to the University of South Florida (USF). Alone that day, I had to move myself into my on-campus housing. I was to have three roommates, each of us having our own room but sharing a bathroom, kitchen, and common living room.

There were lots of cars double-parked, with parents and college students moving boxes. I was walking down the long sidewalk, looking for my building and hoping that I would be able to make friends on campus. I missed my New York friends a lot and wanted to find people to spend time with. That was when I saw this girl walking down the sidewalk. She had a blonde ponytail and was wearing shorts, a T-shirt, and sneakers. I noticed she was carrying a huge box.

I thought to myself, *hey, she looks nice. Maybe we'll meet and become friends*.

Well, I went upstairs to my unit, and there was the girl with the ponytail and big box. She also had both of her parents and an entire camera crew following her and helping her move in—I guess they thought she was nice too. She and her parents had been asked by a local news station to allow them to follow their move-in because they were from Maryland. The station wanted to do a story about the rising costs of out-of-state tuition, and the girl's family had agreed to participate.

I carried in my few boxes and clothes and started setting up my room. I really wanted my bed lofted so that I could have more space in the six-by-eight room, but I didn't have anyone to help me lift the bed. Then the girl sent over the cameraman from the local station to help me. That was how, on move-in day, I met Kathryn, or as her friends and family call her, Kitti—the person who would become my best friend. She and I spent the next four years as roommates.

My story starts with fun memories with friends. I was very fortunate to meet amazing girlfriends who were (and are) strong, funny, and kind women. Kitti finished her degree before me and started looking for work. I remember laughing with her and looking at a newspaper for jobs that she could do with a bachelor's degree in psychology. Kitti ended up working at a private school with children with autism. She made friends with four other women who also worked with kids on the spectrum. Over the years, we all spent hours together at the beach and going out. I didn't know then what I know now—that life was definitely setting me up for a big challenge and change.

Kitti would bring other friends over to hang out at our apartment after work. Or, after going out, we'd chill on the back porch. Those nights that we sat and drank wine and talked were some of my very best nights. Oh, the laughter felt so good.

Out of everyone in the group, I was the only person who wasn't working with children on the spectrum. I was studying secondary education in social studies and history, whereas most of my friends were education or psychology majors. They would tell these stories about how they were hit, kicked, bitten, and screamed at all day. They really loved working with those kids and had the heart to learn and teach. I always knew that something was missing from my own life when they talked about a rough day or told a funny story. I really just thought it was because of the training that they had to teach special needs children.

I never thought that someday I would have the kid with autism, but life had a different plan.

Ten years after that initial move-in day at USF, I had a son. That son would later be diagnosed with autism.

All those fun nights, listening and laughing with friends, feeling like something was missing, have now come full circle.

My missing piece was my son, Max.

Max completed the puzzle because now, as a mother to a child with autism, I see how valuable my friends are in the community.

Finding access to therapy and great therapists is so difficult, but I have this unbelievable team of highly qualified and experienced friends who can support me and give me suggestions to research. I'm forever thankful for all of them and for the continued love and encouragement they give me as a mother.

My friends have given me a gift that they never knew they shared. On those long, dark, wine-filled nights, they taught me compassion, love, patience, and understanding for children with autism. There were things that they didn't understand, but they kept working and learning. It's funny how the world works; I know now why the pieces came together to make me.

I created the blog Ruthfulness in 2012 to help me figure out who I am and what makes me full. I was struggling with my journey and had stopped writing, only to come back at the end of 2016 to start changing my focus and writing my story. My strongest skills, it turns out, are teaching and helping others. Perhaps unsurprisingly, the game I played most as a child was "teacher."

I want my life and my story to continue to be full of friends and family, and I want to continue helping families with children who need early intervention.

Ruthfulness has become a place for parents to located resources to learn about their children's needs, learn how to advocate for their children, and find access to therapy without going broke.

This story is about my journey to become the mom and woman I am today, and the road that led me to embodying everything I learned in a way that allows others to benefit from my experiences.

Chapter 1

BACKGROUND

My parents moved back and forth between New York and Florida during the first four years of my life. My dad worked as a contractor and would move south for work during the colder months. Though I was born and raised in western New York, I spent years living in Florida as a child. Once my brother was born, though, my mother wanted to make sure that we went to school in New York, attended the same school, and had many of the same teachers.

My husband says that I grew up a big fish in a small pond. He also says I'm from Canada because I miss almost all of his pop culture jokes.

I did grow up in a small town that had one school—not like a one-room schoolhouse, but one big building. I really enjoyed school and played three sports in high school. I had leadership positions in different groups and graduated salutatorian of my class.

I gave a speech on graduation day, in June 2000, where I talked about how, no matter where you go and who you become, you always have to remember your community. In the small town I lived in, that was the thing people complained about—everyone knew everyone and their business. At the age of 17, I didn't know that I would desperately search for a community later in my life and would slowly build a strong extended family.

While growing up, I spent a lot of time with my grandparents. My grandma was crazy and full of it when we were growing up. She would always invite extra people over to her house during the holidays, especially if she thought that they didn't have a place or meal to eat. We would have tables from the kitchen through the living room and into the family room. If you showed up late, you would have to walk into the family room, all the way around the tables, to find an empty seat. We had those meals where everyone had to sit and pass the dishes. After all the dishes were finished being passed, you'd holler down the table if you needed something.

When I think about my grandparents, I often think about my marriage. It's easy to grow apart or give up and just divorce, but my grandparents never did that. I think it's romantic that my grandma shouts when she talks to people who are visiting their home so that my hard-of-hearing grandpa can hear what she's saying. She doesn't want him to be left out of the conversation. They'll soon celebrate their 60th anniversary.

Growing up in my small town, I don't remember there being anyone with autism, but we also didn't have any diversity. There was a school in the district that was for handicapped students, but none of them were mainstreamed in our school. So, when I left my hometown, I really had a large learning curve ahead of me.

Once I finished my salutatorian speech about the importance of community, I attended my birthday and graduation parties, and then my parents and brother packed up and moved back to Florida while I chose to stay behind in New York and attend college.

I definitely felt abandoned. When I started classes at a private liberal arts college in August 2000, Mom wasn't going to come back to help move me into college. I had to call and tell her I wanted her there. I explained that parents are there when they send their children to college, and they help set up their room and move in boxes. So, she came to Keuka College and helped. Then she went back to Florida. We only talked on the phone, and I didn't see her on campus ever again.

I played volleyball and loved the college life, traveling back and forth to Florida on breaks. The hardest days to go without a family were when our volleyball team had family night and no one was there to support me. I was honored that the college president stood in as my family on those nights; it helped make me feel included and special.

I was a college student in New York, two thousand miles away from my family, paying out-of-state tuition since my family didn't live in New York anymore, and it was becoming increasingly stressful that I didn't have immediate family in the area. I started considering moving to Florida, but I knew it would mean starting over not knowing anyone, whereas I had lifetime friends in New York. I was offered lots of financial help by Keuka College, as well as plenty of support from my teammates to stay in New York. It was a tough decision, but I ultimately thought that moving was the right decision.

Within a few months of my move to Florida in 2002, my mom ended up leaving my dad. She waited until he left on a trip back to New York to get more stuff, and then she loaded all of her and my brother's things into two cars and left. I got home from my new Florida school one weekend, and she was already moving her stuff into a truck and most of the house was empty. She hadn't told my dad or me. In fact, I had the joy of calling my dad and telling him that she had packed up most of the house and moved out. He cried on the phone and for weeks after. The house stayed pretty empty, minus my room, which was untouched by my mother. I didn't want to be around the sadness and pain and distanced myself further from my mom and dad.

At USF, my new community began. I had the joys of my first live-in boyfriend. I thought I really loved him and wanted to marry him. We shared lots of fun times, but in the end, he wasn't the man I was looking for. After our breakup, I moved back in with Kitti and went to work as a history teacher.

After my bad breakup, I swore off all men. I knew what I wanted, and I gave it to the universe. Maybe I should have been more specific, now that I think about it. I told the universe that I wanted a man who would walk with me in life, encourage me to get up when I fell down, and run with me toward my dreams. That was pretty much all I asked for.

Well, I did get that—and plenty more.

I met Pierce at work and really didn't want to date a colleague; that's always awkward. We became friends first, and he showed me around the county. Over time, I realized that something more was there. I liked just spending time with him.

I still remember when he took me to the beach one weekend. He sat in a chair, and I only had a towel for the sand. After we spent the day together, we walked to the parking lot to go our separate ways. He hugged me and thanked me for hanging out with him. Our cheeks touched, and I felt electricity flow from my cheek all through my body. I couldn't even drive; I needed to calm down first because I couldn't explain or understand the feeling I'd just had from our faces only touching briefly. Not long after that trip, he asked me out to dinner on a "real" date.

I remember our first date over a decade ago on Good Friday. I remember the shirt he wore, the yellow rose he carried, and the restaurant we visited. He still has that shirt!

Several years went by, and we eventually married in the summer of 2009. Celebrating a 50th wedding anniversary at the time, my grandparents made marriage look easy, but it certainly isn't. Moving in together for the first time and learning everything about a person and yourself is a huge challenge.

I believe that marriage is the most challenging thing that I have ever done in my life, and I totally understand why divorce is so common. It's not easy to love and care for another person that has never before been part of your family or community. As newcomers, they have to respect and develop relationships with everyone in your life. In my small-town mind, I just thought that everyone would accept everyone and we would come together with love.

Well, I was totally wrong and had to learn that's not always how things work. Since Pierce and I are an interracial couple, I had to learn to navigate the world of racism. I had to learn the truth about people I had known my entire life and deal with people who didn't want to accept my husband.

In the months leading up to my wedding day, my dad kept refusing to come. I remember crying on my couch in my little one-bedroom apartment about how, after my parents divorced and eventually married other people, I was there for them. I supported their decisions, accepted both of their new spouses, and understood that they wanted to move on and find happiness. All I wanted was the same respect and support.

I asked my grandfather to be my stand-in. I wanted my dad to walk me down the aisle on my wedding day, but I needed my grandpa there to cover if my dad backed out. My dad didn't want to come to my wedding because he would have to see my mom there. He might have to sit near her or be around her at the reception. It was hurtful and seemed to me like he was unable to accept my husband and was trying to find any excuse he could to get out of it.

I didn't invite a certain aunt because she made inappropriate remarks directed at my relationship with Pierce's family. I didn't want a person who didn't know any better to ruin my wedding. It was my husband who said that I needed to invite her and forgive her. He was so kind that I agreed.

It turned out that my dad did show up and both he and my mother put on their civil hats and acted right. It was a great two days of celebration.

After getting married, I definitely had those moments of now what? I thought that everything was going to be easy and life was going to be perfect, but it took a lot of arguing and a lot of searching. I wanted to leave teaching and was searching and searching, going back to college, studying nutrition, taking the MBA exam, and looking for the something that I was missing in my career.

By my fifth year of teaching sixth through twelfth grade history, I realized that there was no growth or development plan that would increase my pay. Teaching seemed like a dead-end road that I had been led down.

After about two years, Pierce and I decided to try for our first baby. Within a few months, we conceived, and our baby arrived at the end of 2011, changing our lives forever.

Chapter 2

BIRTH

During my first pregnancy, I was very active and worked out regularly. I taught group fitness classes at the YMCA until I was 36 weeks pregnant. I also went to prenatal yoga and met some pretty awesome mom friends while I was there.

Overall, the pregnancy was easy.

I was hungry all the time, tired in the afternoons, had minor morning sickness until about 12 weeks, and had huge, swollen ankles during my third trimester.

My husband had never seen childbirth, was nervous about hospitals, and seemed pretty confident he might pass out.

My mom told me she didn't want to be in the room as a support person; she wanted to stay in the waiting room. So, I hired a doula as a coach and asked my aunt

Debbie, a nurse and a second mom to me, to come support me.

Since I was due on October 30, 2011, I stopped working on October 27 and spent the entire weekend walking and doing anything I could to induce labor. I remember when my husband and I were walking in our apartment complex, and he said that he didn't understand why I wasn't in labor if the doctor said that today was my due date. I had to explain that it was a date range and could be any day within the next week or so. At this time, both my husband and I were working as teachers at the same school.

On November 1, I had contractions and called the doula. We walked and walked and then went to the hospital. Once I got to the hospital and was examined, it turned out that I was in false labor. The doula was there, coaching me and giving me an essential oil that was supposed to help the contractions intensify, but it didn't work.

The doctors gave me two choices: either get induced that day or go home, rest, and wait for the "real" labor to begin.

Well, it was pretty painful, this false labor, and because it had stopped, I decided to go home. I was tired and wanted to be in my own bed. I went home, only to find out later that my husband was upset that our son couldn't have 11/1/11 as his birthday.

So, I went home and went to bed and cried for about four hours because I was so uncomfortable and just wanted the baby out of me. I was definitely regretting my decision not to be induced.

That Wednesday night, I couldn't sleep, so I stayed up pacing the hall in general discomfort. I found that resting my body over the kitchen counter on my elbows and swaying from side to side was most soothing. This lasted all Wednesday night into Thursday morning. I continued to shower as that also comforted me. That morning I called my mom and then my aunt.

When my husband got up, he asked how I was doing.

"It feels like false labor again. I'm just going to be home resting for the day."

"Do you want me to stay home with you?" he asked.

"No. I'm fine."

With my assurances, he left for work around 6:00 a.m.

By 7:30 a.m., I was in a lot more pain and had to move into the bedroom.

I decided to call my mom.

"Mom, I'm not sure if this is labor, but I want you to come over."

She lived at least an hour from me. She started on the drive to my house, which ended up taking until almost 9 a.m. I was home alone and in too much pain to time the contractions or get myself to the hospital. Plus, I didn't want to get to the hospital and have to wait hours, only to be told it was false labor again. So I lay in bed and got on all fours when the contractions would come, clenching the pillow or sheets. My mom and aunt would call and time the contractions for me because all I could do was deal with the pain. I never called the doula I was paying. I didn't want her there. I just wanted my mom.

Once my mom arrived, I made her help me put on jeans and a shirt. Then she drove me to the hospital, which was 30 minutes away. I wouldn't let her or my aunt call my husband.

I told them, "Let's get there and make sure this is really happening first."

My aunt, the nurse, said, "Okay, but this is really happening."

I got there and checked into the labor room by 10:30 a.m., and we decided to call my husband at work at about 11:30 a.m.

"We're all at the hospital," my aunt said to him, "and it's for real this time."

Once Pierce arrived around noon, I got the epidural

and had a second epidural when the first one didn't work correctly. They broke my water, and I took a nap. By around 4:30 that afternoon, I was ready to start pushing.

For the next hour and a half, I was monitored and given oxygen.

The nurses kept saying, "The baby's oxygen level is going down."

Due to the pain from the pressure, I struggled with breathing in the oxygen and breathing out. I felt emotional, exhausted, and increasingly uncertain as I wondered if something was wrong with the baby.

I ended up pushing with a group of concerned nurses and doctors around me while they all guessed where the cord was wrapped around the baby. When it was finally delivery time, I was quite shocked when the bed dropped and the doctor stood up and pulled the nine-pound baby out.

It turned out the cord wasn't wrapped around the baby at all. As soon as my son was born, he was taken to the warmer and assessed. He was breathing rapidly and a little shallowly. It seemed like forever that I looked at him, wanting to hold him, but they said I needed to wait a few minutes for his heart rate to stabilize.

During that time, while they cleaned me up, they

examined the cord and found a true knot. A true knot isn't very common because normally a baby with a knotted umbilical cord doesn't survive. I didn't know that at the time and thought it was strange that the nurses asked us if we wanted to keep it. We didn't.

Once I was able to hold our baby, Maximus, his heartbeat and breathing stabilized. He was a miracle, surviving with a true knot and difficult delivery. He was a beautiful baby with jet-black hair that was long enough to twist into a curl on top of his head. He had full, heart-shaped lips with the perfect Cupid's bow. His eyes were closed and he had the longest, thickest eyelashes already. The cutest part was his chubbiness, his chubby cheeks and chubby legs!

I was relieved to finally hold my baby, but I didn't have that hearts-fill-the-room feeling that other women describe. It was more relief that he was in my arms and safe. The most intense feeling of love for me didn't come for my baby. It came when I looked at my husband. We had made this amazing, beautiful baby and had become a family.

Over the next two days, I struggled with breastfeeding but continued to try. Our baby was so quiet and sweet. We were sent home over the weekend and had our first pediatrician appointment the following Monday. I thought the day before that Max looked jaundiced because his color had changed and I could see discoloration in his eyes.

We went to the pediatrician's office and voiced our concerns, but we were taken aback by the nurse practitioner's insecurities regarding the questions we had about our baby. She ordered some tests to confirm his jaundice, but when we asked what the tests would tell us, she changed her mind and said they weren't really necessary. We insisted that we wanted to have them done anyway.

It came down to our guts telling us that we needed to have Max's blood tested to see his bilirubin levels.

It was a weekend, so we went to St. Petersburg General Hospital for the blood test. A nurse performed a heel stick for a blood sample. Before we could get back home, the hospital called us.

"Don't go home," the nurse said. "Go straight to the emergency room at All Children's Hospital."

My heart started racing into overdrive as adrenaline shot through me. I felt pretty unsure of my abilities as a mother, and I was terrified for my baby. I was also physically sore, weak, and experiencing a lot of pain from the delivery.

What followed next marked the first real time I had to advocate for my son's needs.

Chapter 3

NEONATAL INTENSIVE CARE UNIT (NICU)

The emergency room was quite the experience with a newborn.

They took us back right away. While we were in the room, a nurse came and started an IV for our son, and that was when we knew that we would be staying and admitting the baby to the NICU.

I felt vindicated. I had been right that something was wrong with Max—even though he had been born only a few days earlier, I knew my baby.

During the admitting process, my husband and I were in the room and had to answer a lot of questions.

One, in particular, I still remember: the race question.

"What is your child's race?" a nurse asked us.

We looked at each other in confusion. "He's more than one race," we replied.

"I can only check one box."

After a long discussion on the long list of choices, Pierce and I decided not to answer. So, on some of the hospital paperwork, it says our son is white, and on some of the paperwork, it says he's black. That's because, depending on the parent that was present, the hospital employee would just put the parent's race for the child.

Once we were upstairs in the NICU, we weren't able to hold Maximus. We were told that his jaundice level was 27, which was considered life-threatening for a three-day-old baby.

They didn't feed him during that entire first day; they only gave him IV fluids and lights. He screamed through the night. I only know because my husband told me—he stayed. The doctors told me to go home and rest. I know they asked me to go home because I wouldn't have been able to handle him crying all night.

As time went by and I kept trying to pump and was only getting an ounce and a half each time, I started to read and ask questions about the jaundice.

I learned the number-one way to help a baby with jaundice is to flush the system with as many fluids as possible, which meant feeding the baby with more than IV fluids.

On the second and third day, they gave him all of the breast milk that I could make. I sat on ice for days and could hardly walk from the parking garage to the NICU floor. There was no bed in the NICU, only a chair. I would go home for a few hours, then come back, and I had to be driven by a family member each way.

On the morning of the fourth day in the NICU, I said that I wasn't making any more milk from just pumping. Without holding the baby to feed him, I needed formula to supplement his needs because my body couldn't keep up.

My husband had to threaten to walk out of the hospital with our son against medical advice if they didn't get us the formula.

Within 24 hours, Max was recovering much faster and needed less phototherapy.

After five days in the NICU, we were able to take our baby home again. They said after running many tests that they didn't believe that Max had suffered any brain damage or loss of hearing from the event.

The entire five days were very stressful for me as a new mom. I wasn't able to sleep, I wasn't making enough breast milk, and I was physically sore from labor and had not fully rested after the delivery.

Once we were home and settled, we discovered that the formula was excellent for feeding a big baby.

I had maternity leave with Max until late January. As the end of my maternity leave approached, my husband pleaded with me to quit my job and continue to stay home. He was teaching full-time while trying to get his photography business off the ground. He asked me to stay home with the baby and work on emails, calls, and sales for his photography business. I said no.

I can say now that I, one hundred percent, without doubt or hesitation, regret this decision.

I loved my baby, but I thought there would be this instant love and hearts would fill the room when I gave birth to him, and that didn't happen.

What did happen was I discovered a more profound love and deeper connection with my husband. I didn't realize at the time that when I said no it would permanently alter my relationship and marriage with my husband.

Ultimately, my husband knew what I needed and what our son was going to need. I, however, was not in a clear state of mind and was under high amounts of stress. I don't have much memory of the time I spent with my son after we came home from the hospital.

It wasn't until February, when I was back at work, that a cloud lifted.

I was walking down our open concourse and, as I was returning to my classroom, it was like a fog lifted. I immediately realized where I was and then thought, "Shit, what have I been doing?"

I would assume that I had some form of postpartum depression or, as a therapist told me, maybe even post-traumatic stress disorder (PTSD).

I had to see a therapist from my work employee assistance program because of the amount of marriage stress we were experiencing. After rejecting Pierce's idea to stay home with our son, we started fighting all the time. I wasn't happy. He wasn't happy. We weren't meeting each other's relationship needs, but I didn't want to be left or leave him. I really loved him and wanted to figure out what was upsetting him, so I went to counseling by myself.

I had to work through a lot of issues, and the fact that I couldn't remember months after the birth of my son compounded the issues and stresses in all aspects of my life. Nine months after I went back to work, my husband quit teaching to pursue his photography business full-time. My marriage continued to have ups and downs as we worked through the next several years.

When I went back to work in 2012, my mother-in-law started taking care of my son.

Max grew into a happy toddler, making baby sounds and noises, meeting milestones within ranges. He seemed to be developing normally, crawling at 10 months and walking at 12. He was great at taking pictures, always laughing and smiling. He interacted well with adults and loved to be among family. We would take him to the library, children's museum, and on trips to see family. He slept well and rarely cried. Our only struggle before the age of one was tummy time—Max would cry when you made him lie on his stomach.

Some of the most beautiful pictures I have of Max are from these early years. You can see him look right at my husband behind the camera. You can see the light in his eyes and the happiness in his smile.

It wasn't until he was about 15 to 18 months that I started to notice some behavioral concerns. That was around the time that Max received several vaccines. I had read up on the MMR (measles, mumps, and rubella) vaccine and we had decided not to give him this vaccine at 12 months because, although his development had been charting normally, he was making sounds and signs but not many words. At 12 months they also want to give other vaccines. I didn't like that so many shots or vaccines were given at one time and opted to wait until 15 months.

The conversation goes around and around regarding any link between autism and vaccines, but in terms of noticeable behavior and communication concerns, that was when I noticed a change.

Around this time, my mother-in-law stopped watching him, partly because he was more difficult to deal with and so very active. We joke that Max crawled until he could run. Then he never stopped running. The other factor was that my sister-in-law had a baby in July and needed help taking care of her infant.

We knew that caring for both an infant and my active 18-month-old would be too much for my mother-in-law, so we put Max in a day care near where I worked.

He did fine in the day care and moved into the two's class. At that time, staff started to report that he was biting his peers. He would wrestle and bite someone on the arm or back. There was also a day when he bit a girl's finger because she was telling on him for putting acorns in his pockets and mouth. So, he decided to bite her finger that was in his face because he didn't want to get into trouble.

At that point, Max was only parallel playing and not speaking. He would sit next to other children who were doing the same activity, but wouldn't play with or interact with his peers. His favorite game was filling and dumping. You would watch him repeatedly fill a container with toys and then dump them all out. He was also very sensory seeking. Max had to constantly be moving, jumping, climbing or swinging. He was constantly seeking ways to get pressure or any movement to and on his body. He would jump on furniture, jump off furniture, climb anything and enjoyed swinging back and forth. He also had strong oral concerns. Max would drool until his shirt was wet. He also chewed his shirt collar and any hard object he could find.

Since he wasn't potty-trained at two and was still in diapers, we had some problems at day care.

I remember the afternoon that I picked him up and he was wet all over. He didn't have a diaper on for naptime. Max had wet the entire bed. When I asked why, no one had an answer. They blamed him and said that he must have gone into the bathroom, taken the diaper off, and pulled his pants back up all by himself.

A few weeks later, I picked him up to take him home. We made it to the car and when I went to put him in his car seat, I smelled poop. This time, I took pictures of his bottom and the diaper because he had pooped and no one had changed him. I knew he had to have been sitting in the dirty diaper a while because the skin on his butt was open and bleeding. Again, I received no answers or apologies, but they gave plenty of excuses about a two-year-old not letting them know that he had to go to the bathroom, even though they had regular bathroom checks every hour.

I was so angry that adults would make the problem a toddler's fault. I was paying them to be responsible for caring for my child and felt like my son was being neglected. The other children seemed happy and cared for, so why was my son not getting the same treatment?

The final issue was related to the biting again—that ended our stay at this day care. The director and teacher wanted to write up Max for biting; however, my son never left a mark or broke the skin on another child. And yet I always had to sign an incident report about my child's behavior.

Then, one day after I had picked up Max without any negative reports, I noticed a broken and bruised bite on the back of his left arm. I took pictures of his arm and immediately contacted the director. I also made an appointment to speak with the co-owner about the day care's failure to file an incident report. After the director and co-owner looked into my concerns, they came back with additional excuses as to why the incident was not properly documented.

They'd say things like, "The teacher was moved to help cover another room, so she wasn't in there. There was a substitute." Then, they would word the situation so that the story negatively portrayed my child. "Well,

Max was playing in housekeeping when the student took the toy he was playing with, so Max tried to bite him. Max needs to use his words."

Did I get an incident report or any feedback from the teacher? Nope. It made me feel like my child was being watched and singled out for behaviors, but if another child bit him back, then it was somehow acceptable.

While Max was at this day care, I delivered our second child. I went back to work in January 2014 and continued to breastfeed and pump at work while my mother-in-law watched our new baby, Social. She was a good baby who was most often carried because I would have to run and chase after Max. He didn't really notice or pay attention to his sister. He wasn't talking or expressing himself during this time, so he just acted like she wasn't there.

Max was so difficult and challenging while I had a young baby to care for. He was running and climbing all the time—sometimes falling and getting concussions!

He said very few words and wasn't able to make requests for what he wanted. I tried very hard to anticipate his needs and make sure he was always happy and taken care of. I thought I was doing what a good mom should do. However, I was actually making his communication worse.

Since I always anticipated his needs and knew a natural schedule of things that he liked, I could keep him from getting upset. Once he wanted something that I couldn't understand, his demands would increase, and the frustration would begin—then he would become upset. If I couldn't determine what he needed or wanted, then he would cry and scream, kick and hit. It was terrible and I often felt like I needed to try to keep Max happy. If he was happy, then managing life was much easier.

After my daughter was born and my son was close to turning two, my husband would spend hours working at night for his photography business by going to marketing events and participating in an entrepreneur training program. I would come home from work and have to manage the evenings with the kids until he returned at bedtime. My goal was just to keep Max happy and calm so that I could pick up the kids, cook for them, bathe them, and put them in bed.

During our newborn training class, we were told that if we couldn't take the screaming anymore and thought we might hurt our baby, we should put the baby down in his or her crib, walk away, and shut the door. Then, once we'd calmed ourselves down, we could resume trying to care for our baby. That was part of the shaken baby training portion of class. For some reason, it stuck with me, and I thought that if I didn't know what to do, I could try that. When I couldn't get Max to stop screaming, I would put him into the bed and close the door. He would roll around on his bed, jump on the bed, cry, and sometimes fall asleep. Well, sure enough, it did work—and, to a degree, we still use it. We all need time to cool down, calm down, and regroup to solve a problem. Then, when calm, we can talk about what happened and what we need.

After having my daughter, I taught StrollerStrides (a mommy and me stroller fitness class). I made friends with other moms and children similar in age to both my children. Because we were out in groups, I could see that my son acted differently than their boys. His tantrums weren't like real tantrums—they were more frequent and severe. Everyone tried to just blame the terrible twos. But, deep down, I knew that this was something completely different.

When I called my USF friends and told them about Max's behavior, they were always supportive but didn't want to make judgments without observing him with their own eyes. They didn't live close enough to visit, but they always offered a listening ear and recommendations for reading or research.

Chapter 4

PRIVATE PRESCHOOL

During this time of lots of tantrums and problems at home, Max was still in the day care where we were having issues with biting and diaper changing.

Since I have an education degree and plenty of teacher friends, they suggested I try to get help from his day care or the county's Early Steps program. So, I tried to get services for speech through Early Steps of Pinellas, which provides free therapy to children under the age of three who have developmental delays.

When Max was almost two and a half years old, I took him to be evaluated with the Battelle Developmental Inventory (BDI-2). The BDI-2 is a developmental assessment used for infants and young children. He. Even though Max was only making a few sounds and having trouble with particular skills, he didn't qualify for services. I found out that he had to be two standard deviations below the target range for a two-year-old in order to qualify for therapy. The only thing I could do was wait six months to have him reevaluated.

This was one of my first experiences with evaluations. I learned that, as a parent, the less you answer or the more you give negative complaints or descriptions of development, the better it is for your child. If you believe that your child needs developmental therapy or support, but may not have a severe deficit, then saying no to more questions— instead of explaining how your child does some part of the developmental milestone—is actually better because you will increase your child's score, thereby qualifying for assistance. The program helps the worst-affected children first, those with the greatest need. If you need free services, then your child has to score two standard deviations below their developmental age.

When I mentioned the evaluation to the day-care staff, they didn't seem to notice or say anything about my concerns. I thought that was odd because they were the experts on development and responsible for recommending children for evaluation.

It was at that point when we started looking for new schools. We temporarily moved Max to a different school for better care, and then we enrolled him in a private preschool by our house.

The temporary day care alerted me to the previous day care's incompetence. They were able to explain the system and their responsibility to have conversations with parents.

Max started private preschool with Ms. Natalie while he was still two. This was now his third day care in one full calendar year. My husband was no longer working a full-time job as a teacher. I had just had our daughter in October and was back to working full-time. Our daughter was staying with her grandma and cousin during the day while I was working.

We selected the private preschool because of the technology, staff, and outside time. It was also only one mile from my mother-in-law's house. We wanted to be part of a community where we could get Max help as needed and trust the teacher and staff involved in his care. One big problem with the other two day cares had been that the same people were not consistently in the room each day. There could be a main teacher, but her hours might be cut or reduced if the numbers of children were down. Then, a teacher from another classroom would shift to cover my son's class, or my son would be moved into a different class if his peers left early for the day. It appeared that those changes were too much for our son.

At the private school, Max would have the same two teachers all day. We thought that this would open us up to real professional opinions and suggestions about our child's actions, behaviors, and skills based on an entire day. Max started at the new school, and we had high hopes that we would be able to build a foundation to help him.

Within 10 days, Max received 14 incident reports from the school. The most common problems were biting and injuries that occurred from him running off.

Pierce and I were not surprised and knew that there would be an adjustment period for Max at the new school because the school had higher expectations for their students (even at age two). It was different from the last day care because the information we were receiving was consistent and unbiased.

Hearing the teachers' concerns and complaints, I started noticing some other differences in comparison to my friends' children. Max didn't have the language skills, play skills, or eye contact that other children had. He seemed to be in his own world; he just wanted to watch and play by himself.

When my daughter was born, his behaviors became more than a terrible two-year-old's.

If I didn't know what he wanted, he would start screaming and kicking for what appeared to be no reason. He would become inconsolable, and no one knew how to help him. Max would drool through three shirts a day because he was putting the collar of his shirt in his mouth, and he would only eat particular foods, always with sauce. He wouldn't allow me to brush his teeth, which eventually led to major dental work. He wasn't able to follow basic directions, would fall down often, was climbing and jumping nonstop, and had the hardest time going to sleep.

Oh, and I forgot the running, running, and running. That kid could run!

One of the more difficult behaviors was at bedtime and after school. I would be home by myself most nights with both kids. Max was so busy and crazy. Then, if I couldn't understand what he wanted, he would scream and kick the floor. He would take a bath alone fine but often was dangerous in the tub with his sister or when climbing into the bath alone. At 18 months, he smashed his two front teeth while in the bath.

I was so exhausted from the battle and struggle every night with Max that I trusted the advice his school was offering. The school suggested that Max did have a developmental delay and that he could benefit from more help and services. My son passively refused to participate in the school's assessment and instead washed his hands over and over, so we decided to contact Pinellas Association for Retarded Children (PARC) and Early Steps again.

Chapter 5

FIRST EVALUATION

In September, I reached out to the Early Steps case manager I'd met in April when Max hadn't qualified for services. I described all of the difficult problems that I was having at home, as well as the school's concerns. She explained that Early Steps ended at age three and Florida Diagnostic and Learning Resource System (FDLRS) took over and could offer services. She said she could schedule the reevaluation to determine whether Max was eligible to qualify through FDLRS. Our evaluation was on October 1, 2014, and our final determination meeting was October 20.

While I worked on the county programs for early intervention, the school director paired me with other parents who had gone through the program. He also set up an appointment for PARC to evaluate and provide services until we could go through the process.

Ms. Virginia visited us on October 9 and evaluated Max at his private preschool. She sent home a report that looked at cognitive, language, fine motor, gross motor, social emotional, and self-help skills. Max did not assess well, which allowed us to start early intervention.

Ms. Virginia determined that she could help him for one hour a week under the Family Focus Program. I was so happy to finally have feedback from someone who was so kind and willing to help my son. The PARC program was the first to help us.

The Family Focus Program, for children aged birth to six years, is funded by the Juvenile Welfare Board (JWB). The once-a-week therapy is provided at home or in school. The evaluation process is simple and takes just one hour for the therapist to complete. You, as the parent, will get a copy of all the forms completed. There is a lot of paperwork to fill out—just do it!

Once the child is receiving services, parents will have direct contact with a professional early intervention specialist. This was excellent for me when my son was two. I was trying so hard to find him help and kept running into dead-ends. Finally, when he started to see Ms. Virginia and I had detailed weekly reports about what my child was and was not able to do, I had the key words and evidence to keep pursuing additional help.

Some of the activities I read in the reports included

color recognition, shapes, lacing beads, identifying cognitive concepts, communication, and many general development skills. Ms. Virginia was always helpful in leaving notes about which activities my child enjoyed and which were challenging that day. She always noted when he was successful, and they celebrated together. Obviously, at this time, we didn't know that my son had autism, but we knew that he wasn't speaking and was struggling with developmental educational milestones. If it hadn't been for the private preschool and the services provided by the PARC Family Focus Program, I would not have been able to get additional early intervention detection, screenings, and services for my son.

Early Steps ends at age three, and that's when Florida Diagnostic and Learning Resource System (FDLRS) takes over. So, we went back to Early Steps and explained what the problems were now. Max turned three that November. He qualified for help, so we entered Early Steps and scheduled the meeting to discuss a plan for his education and services. He then qualified as developmentally delayed for the primary exceptionality with language impaired (LI) as a secondary category or other program and service area. The program was able to quickly enroll us in school-based services. We had a meeting to discuss putting Max in a blended ESE pre-k classroom. There he would have an Individualized Education Plan (IEP) and receive speech therapy.

FDLRS was very thorough in evaluating Max. We had to do a hearing screening even though we had one after Max's stay in the NICU. The hearing test was free, but it was quite the experience.

I had to sit in the padded room with him where he took the test. It didn't seem like he passed, but apparently, he did just fine. Max was able to do the parts of the test that required verbal responses—he just really didn't want to wear any headphones. Sometimes, I think that he really is hard of hearing because he doesn't respond or repeat back words, but they're the experts and said he could hear. Once we had a pass on the hearing test, we went to our meeting about Max's placement. At our meeting, I remember the words "spectrum" and "autism-like behavior" being mentioned, but they were subtle.

This would now be the fourth classroom environment for him within a calendar year. I felt like a terrible mom and didn't think that I was doing anything right. I didn't know what was wrong with my child. More importantly, I felt like I didn't know what I could do to help him. There were days that I wondered why I had this child. I would think to myself that he needed and deserved a better mother than me, someone who could help him. I felt that Max definitely had a sensory processing disorder (SPD). During the period while Max still didn't qualify for help, I read and researched whatever I saw and could describe. When I read the SPD information on spdstar.org, I realized Max had nine out of 10 of the items on the list.

The preschool checklist for SPD, found at spdstar.org/basic/symptoms-checklist, now has 14 items.

1. My child has difficulty being toilet trained.

2. My child is overly sensitive to stimulation, overreacts to or does not like touch, noise, smells, etc.

3. My child is unaware of being touched/bumped unless done with extreme force/intensity.

4. My child is in constant motion.

5. My child has difficulty learning and/or avoids performing fine-motor tasks such as using crayons and fasteners on clothing.

6. My child seems unsure how to move his/her body in space, is clumsy, and awkward.

7. My child is intense, demanding, or hard to calm and has difficulty with transitions.

8. It is hard to understand my child's speech.

9. My child has difficulty making friends (overly aggressive or passive/withdrawn).

10. My child does not seem to understand verbal instructions.

11. My child is in constant motion.

12. My child gets in everyone else's space and/or touches everything around him.

13. My child has sudden mood changes and temper tantrums that are unexpected.

14. My child seems weak, slumps when sitting/standing, prefers sedentary activities.

I kept reading and reading. I asked questions of other professionals and even parents. No one on the FDLRS panel suggested that we get a developmental pediatrician's diagnosis or even further evaluations— they just kept on with their suggested services and continued drafting his original and first IEP.

During this time, my husband would attend for support. He listened to my concerns and understood that I really thought Max was developmentally delayed. He believed in me and wanted to make sure that his voice as a father could be heard each time Max was evaluated.

We decided at the October 20 meeting that we would change schools again and place Max at the elementary school closest to my in-laws' house, which was the same school my husband had attended. Pierce advocated for the school because his mother had years of experience volunteering through the school and state as a social worker. We met the teacher and she suggested January as the best time to start Max at the new school.

Chapter 6

PUBLIC PRESCHOOL

Then, on Wednesday, November 12, my mother-in-law called as I was driving home to tell me that she could no longer watch our daughter, Social.

I remember asking her, "Okay, well, when does this take effect?"

And she said, "Today."

My mother-in-law was having some health concerns and some testing done, and she had called to cancel permanently because they suspected that she had cancer.

I had to immediately start calling and searching for a place for Social to go. My husband and I took turns taking days off work until I found a place that would let me enroll her part-time. I went back to the last learning place that Max had been for the summer and explained that I was in desperate need of childcare for a one-year-old. The classroom didn't have a full-time space. However, I could bring Social when another child who was attending part-time was out. Every two weeks, the program director would tell me what days my daughter could attend. She would go at least three days a week, and my husband would help out as much as he could during the day and work at night. In addition to his full-time photography business, Pierce had to work a part-time job at a patent law office to help us cover our costs for a few years.

At the end of November, near Thanksgiving, we learned that Glenda, my mother-in-law, did have cancer in her abdomen, but doctors weren't sure how advanced it was yet. She was scheduled for surgery at the beginning of December.

She went in for surgery and ended up staying in the hospital for three weeks. They were able to remove almost all of the cancerous mass, but then there were two additional bowel obstructions that had to be corrected after the initial surgery. Glenda went home right before Christmas and still needed a lot of care. It took six months of recovery before she could even start the chemotherapy portion of her treatment.

During the month that Glenda was in the hospital, I hardly ever saw my husband. He would work from her room, come back to pick up our son from school, and then leave within the hour that I got home. It was very difficult on us all. Obviously, everyone deals with sickness differently, but I wasn't expecting my husband to shut me out as much as he did. He only let me visit Glenda once while she was in the hospital. He never wanted to talk about it and only once went off on me about the stress.

Due to my mother-in-law's sickness, having to place my daughter in day care, and my husband cutting back on work to take care of his mom and Max, we had to move up Max's start time at the elementary school. We called everyone, including the teacher, and told them that situations had changed and that we needed to start Max in December. It wasn't the plan, but we as a family were just trying to make things survivable.

Once Max entered the school program, we realized it was very different than what we'd previously experienced.

Public school turned out to be very disheartening.

I have had to fight back a lot of fear in writing about the experiences I had as the parent of a child with special needs because of how painful and wrong it was for Max.

My child has no voice—he is a nonverbal three-year-old, four-year-old, five-year-old who does not come home to tell me about his day. I don't know when or if he ever will.

I had to decide that, through my pain and experience, I would eventually find a way to help others going through similar things.

In December, Max started at the public elementary school with Ms. Rosalyn and Ms. Miller.

The Early Childhood Intervention team from Max's qualifying assessment told me to expect a lot of things, but nothing was as described. Max was one month from turning three, which is when the Early Childhood Intervention team transitions from at-home or at-school therapy for students under three to using the public preschool programs to provide a blended learning environment with special education services and therapy.

Though we met with Ms. Miller before Max entered the school, the communication and understanding with her were not present. Max was in school for the full month of December before he even started to receive services for his speech.

Later, we would also have occupational therapy (OT) added to his list of services. Max was not potty-trained and had just turned three. I was sending Pull-Ups and wipes as well as other extra clothing. He wasn't speaking at this time; he said about 10 to 25 words that were difficult to understand if you didn't know him.

Max would come home from school and there would be notes like "Had a great day! ☺"

As a parent, I couldn't help but wonder, *what the hell does that mean?*

I kept asking questions and wanting more information. I also kept saying that this wasn't what the district had told us. I had to keep asking for information to the point that we had to have a conference.

Now, I always recommend all parents with young children with an IEP ask for an immediate conference the first week of school in order to establish clear expectations and needs. The teachers were very nice— maybe too nice. Ms. Miller would say, "He's fine. Don't worry."

The problem was that all I did was worry. Max had been in three day cares within the year and was now headed for a fourth. At the private preschool that had helped us so much, I had been sent detailed notes about his day and plenty of incident reports. I was so used to regular feedback with the teacher about how he was doing and what he was struggling with that now it was a huge shock.

I knew my son couldn't be that different from one environment to another because I had seen how terribly he'd transitioned in the past. Once we got through conference number two and had established some demands on communication, some things started to improve.

As the months went on, Ms. Miller and Ms. Rosalyn could see that we weren't out to question their every lesson or plan for the day but that our son really needed help and we didn't have a medical diagnosis as to what the problem was.

At our meeting, several people mentioned that he had spectrum behavior. I knew that was most likely true, but my family really needed help from professionals that knew how to work with children with developmental delays.

We thought that if we got him early intervention, then he would have a better chance at success moving forward. I really rode the teachers hard those first six months and demanded the information I needed to seek more help for my son.

Part of the solution was that we, as the adults, needed to try to walk in each other's shoes. Once Ms. Rosalyn and Ms. Miller could see how we worked with our son and how much we needed to know about his specific daily actions and behaviors, they started to see that we valued their help and communication.

During those six months that Max was in the new program at the public school, we continued to work on appointments to find out what else we could do to help him. Max had a private speech evaluation at All Children's Hospital on November 13, 2014. This was just weeks before we knew we were going to start him in the public school program where he would receive speech therapy.

When the speech evaluation was complete, and two sessions were recommended weekly, I asked to schedule appointments. The staff was unable to do that because the hospital didn't have any therapists available.

By this time, I had already called repeatedly to get an OT appointment and a developmental pediatrician appointment for a diagnosis. My concern with getting the diagnosis was that I knew it would help with insurance. My insurance company would only cover 60 speech and OT visits without the diagnosis. At this point, we knew that Max needed a lot of speech therapy and language therapy to start getting him to speak. However, we couldn't find a therapist in our county. We had hit a roadblock.

Chapter 7

APPOINTMENTS

During my Thanksgiving break, while Glenda was being diagnosed with cancer and we were waiting to start Max in the new school, I learned that the children's hospital had a six-month-plus waiting list to see a developmental pediatrician.

I was referred to a doctor in Tampa as a way to speed up the process and get a diagnosis. This doctor came highly recommended and, when I called, he had availability!

Yes, availability within two weeks ... because you had to pay out of pocket, no insurance.

It would cost a minimum of $750 to $1,000. If you needed a follow-up appointment or additional testing, then the cost went up from there. A lot of people go to this doctor and pay his price because of how terrible access is for a developmental pediatrician in Pinellas County.

But, by this point, spending that kind of money was out of the question for us. I was paying for day care at a premium price, and my husband couldn't work many hours at his part-time job doing research for the patent law office because he was taking Max to and from school, as well as staying at the hospital with his mom.

So, I had to keep looking for doctors.

One day, I was sitting and brainstorming where to look next when I thought about the University of South Florida. Since I'd graduated from there, I knew that they had a large medical center.

I looked up their youth services and searched for developmental pediatricians. It turned out they would take our insurance, and I could get an appointment within three months, so we set up an appointment for April 20, 2015.

While at the speech evaluation at All Children's Hospital, we were able to get an OT evaluation on April 2. The appointments were stacking up, stress was high, and work was demanding. My mother-in-law was very sick, I was late to work almost every day, and we were financially struggling.

I got a letter in my file at work because of how often I rushed in late. My administrator asked me why I was frequently late and when I told him, he looked down at his desk. He said, "Why didn't you tell us that you were going through this?"

My response was, "What were you going to do about it?"

I had to sign that letter, and I still have a copy in my desk at work. It's a reminder of what I was going through and how, even when you don't want to talk to others above you about your life problems, sometimes it can do you some good, or maybe prevent a letter from going into your permanent file.

My husband hardly talked to me anymore. He spent most evenings working or caring for his mother. It left me alone nightly in our small, cramped apartment taking care of the kids, making dinner, and trying to do bedtime.

I failed at keeping anything clean. My husband was still working on developing his business, and I was trying to help by sending emails and making calls for more contacts.

We didn't have a working dishwasher in our apartment or a washing machine or dryer. I did laundry on the weekend with everyone else in our complex. It was about six to eight loads a week and would cost at least $20 or $30.

I would load up a large garbage can that we used as a hamper, push it in front of me with all the laundry soap, and pull the kids in a wagon behind me. Max would run out of the laundry room, dig in the "ashtray" dirt (that's what I called the dirt outside the laundry room because everyone put their cigarettes out there instead of the trash), climb the stairs, or just start opening other people's dryers.

Our dining room had carpet, and it was gross, so I had to feed the kids at one of those IKEA kids' tables in the kitchen. Most nights I sat at the kiddie table and had dinner. We also had Pierce's business running out of our apartment. We had boxes, bags, and bins in every corner.

All the while, I still kept pushing for more help and more answers. When we had our OT appointment at All Children's Hospital, the therapist was so kind. It was so nice to have her see what my concerns were and how Max was physically all over the place with his activity level.

Then there was the drooling and mouthing of things at three years old. She definitely recommended therapy twice a week, and she spent about 10 minutes showing me how to use a brushing protocol on Max to help him calm down.

She provided a plastic, rectangular comb and showed me how to take the brush and give strokes down his arm or leg. After 10 strokes, she showed me how to safely give joint compressions by bending and holding his elbow, knee, or ankle and giving pressure to the joint. I would hold, squeeze, count to three, and release. Then, I'd repeat that three times and give 10 more brushes. I have seen many similar techniques and variations of this protocol.

Once we found what worked, we would modify as needed. Sometimes joint compressions were not needed, or sometimes we needed a lot of compressions and less brushing. We also learned how to do this without the brush—if we were out of the house, I had to learn how to calm Max even if I didn't have the specific tools.

It really helped, and even though I wasn't doing it exactly like a trained occupational therapist, it was a tool that I could implement to calm Max's sensory system when he was too worked up or couldn't sleep.

The therapist told me he really needed help and that I should take her report and go somewhere else. She said that their facility had so many children who needed clinic assessments that they didn't have enough therapists and availability to schedule everyone. The waiting list was so long that they weren't adding more names. I took the information she gave me and went home to implement what I could.

On April 20, my husband and I picked up Max from school and drove him to the USF medical center in Tampa. It's about a 45-minute drive without rush-hour traffic. I don't remember taking Social with us, but I also don't remember who would have watched her. So, she must have been with us.

We met with a doctor about our concerns and interest in doing the autism testing. She watched Max and gave us some suggestions. She said because he was still three and just starting in school with therapy that we should consider doing additional therapy for his speech. We had insurance and would have to find a way to pay for it.

She recommended that we take a wait-and-see approach. She could see where Max did certain things that would suggest autism, but the rate of diagnosis had most recently skyrocketed and she wanted to make sure the diagnosis was accurate. So, we left there like, "Okay! Here we go!"

I found a therapy clinic that had availability and could offer both speech and OT that took our insurance. It was in South Tampa, 19 miles away, over the bridge, and onto the toll road. I would have to travel the route on weekdays between the hours of 3:30 and 6:00 p.m.

Our first appointment was May 5. In order to get Max started, I had to take appointment times in the middle of the day, meaning I had to take off from work. I missed a lot of work and therefore had no money.

Max's first day of therapy was May 26. I drove 14 miles to pick Max up and then drove another 20 miles to Tampa. I had to pay by Toll-By-Plate or take the busy highway. Then I stayed for 30 minutes of therapy only to have to turn around afterward and drive the 20 miles home.

We did that for six months to see if we saw any progress. We did! Max showed huge gains and improvements. Even so, Max was on the verge of turning four and we were still having some major sensory problems at home and school. I was able to get his next evaluation and therapy appointment on the same day of the week, so we could make the trip just once a week for both speech and OT. We would do this for over a year, until January 2017.

Chapter 8

DENTIST

I almost forgot about the dentist.

When Max was little, he would always bite down whenever I used a washcloth to wipe his gums or used one of those rubber brushes that you put on your finger and stick in your kid's mouth.

As he got older, brushing his teeth became a huge ordeal. He loved to chew on things that didn't belong in his mouth, but when the toothbrush went in, he would freak, then run and scream.

I was a regular mom with a lot on her plate at the time, and I struggled to get through the 8:00 p.m. crying and colic fits that my daughter would have for the first six months of her life. As such, I did a really poor job of regularly restraining my toddler son so I could brush his teeth.

I would have to lay him down on the hallway floor outside the bathroom and hold him down with my body so that I could pry open his mouth with one hand and brush with the other hand. It was a nightmare. If my husband was home from work, then I had help, but most nights it was just me getting the kids ready for bed.

I cringe just thinking about how terrible it was.

I asked other people, googled what to do, and researched brushes and things to help but found no real answers. As Max was getting closer to three and we were looking for all the help we could get and had started the process to enter the public school, I also started working on finding a dentist.

I searched out recommendations and made an appointment.

Going into the appointment, I was honest and up-front about my concerns. I talked about how my son had a lot of sensory problems and that brushing was very, very difficult. I explained that he might scream and get scared and asked if I could go back with him in case he needed to be held.

You've probably heard those horror stories about the kids that wiggle, scream, and won't hold still, so much that they end up with a dislocated shoulder or other major injury because a technician tried to restrain them.

I was very nervous and scheduled an appointment near lunchtime so that fewer children would be in the office. I again had to take time off of work to make the appointment. We went to a female dentist in our town and were extremely upset with how things went at the appointment.

My son did exactly what I had told the office he would do—he cried, screamed, and resisted. I went back with him to the chair to have the exam and cleaning done. The hygienist did the best she could but had to have the dentist come over and examine his mouth.

When she came over, he was, of course, screaming in terror. She looked in his mouth and said he needed to stop screaming. I tried to calm him but knew that was not going to happen and that we needed to get the hell out of that place. I tried to explain since, clearly, her office staff had done zero to consult with us prior to our appointment.

She then repeated, "He needs to stop screaming because he is giving me a headache."

Then she excused herself from my son's appointment and said she had to go because he was making other patients in the back nervous. I was able to calm him down and then she returned to lecture me about food and his diet. She told me what to feed him and what to avoid because of how it would give him cavities.

I replied, "Okay. What about his mouth and cavities now?"

She proceeded to tell me that she couldn't do the work on his mouth. *What the hell?!*

"Why do you think I came here?" I asked. "I was told that you do sedation dentistry and could fix his teeth."

She then told me that she would recommend a dentist in Bradenton. Bradenton is a 30-minute drive south over the Skyway Bridge.

At this point, I was ready to cry in her office but was so pissed off that I couldn't show my weakness. When I left, I told the receptionist how angry I was about the way we had been treated and informed her that I was not going to return or pay for that visit. She billed my insurance, and I didn't see another bill with anything additional I owed.

The only way I ever get a sense of justice about that incident is when I tell other moms not to go there because the dentist was not kind but condescending.

I spent the next few weeks working on cleaning and brushing Max's teeth as best I could—then I tossed the lady's dietary advice right out the window with her shitty attitude.

I asked my own dentist for advice and she gave us some great tips about working with a wet washcloth on one side of his mouth to bite down on or trying to use a bite block. She even gave us one to test.

Max had to miss school the day he saw this dentist, and I confided in Ms. Miller that his teeth were bad and I really wanted to get them fixed. I shared how terrible our experience had been, how the dentist had talked to me about my son, and how she'd handled the situation. She was shocked but was able to give me the name of a local pediatric dentist she had previously recommended who several of her students had used in the past.

I called the pediatric dentist and gave the same speech I had given the first terrible dentist. This time, I received a different response.

She said, "Okay, no problem. Just to let you know, we don't like for parents to go back for examinations, but if it makes you and your child more comfortable, then we will have you come back."

They also had a separate waiting room for special needs children and their families. It was like a dream come true for a doctor's/dentist's office. There were all kinds of different chairs and books. There was a video screen to watch a welcome video and one or two simple toys. We could wait in there for Max's appointments and consultations, and he could lie on the floor or do whatever he felt like doing. Then, when it was time to go in, he could walk behind the desk area and around to the examination rooms without having to see any of the other children or parents waiting.

I was able to go back with Max because of how bad the first visit to the dentist had been for him. This dentist knew that she had to overcome and fix the damage that the first dentist had done to my child.

Everything was very different this time. The dentist and the assistant were very kind and soft-spoken. They explained everything that they would do and had a tablet for Max to play on.

We found out that every back tooth needed some kind of repair, nothing severe, but they were still in need of fixing so that he could keep his teeth and not be in pain.

I had to have a consult about the cost and what insurance would and would not pay for. Insurance would not cover the sedation—we knew that we needed sedation because of his sensory problems. The total cost was $745 for the sedation by a board-certified anesthesiologist and $711.45 for the actual dental work. That included having to pay for another dental exam and x-rays within the calendar year.

I had to call the anesthesiology office and pay a minimum of $250 30 days prior to the appointment to guarantee the procedure. That ended up being a super big pain in my butt with insurance six months after the procedure was done. Since I paid $500 off my flexible spending card, but Max hadn't yet had the service when I turned in the documentation and paperwork, the insurance company wanted me to pay back the $500. I'm pretty sure I screamed, cried, and pleaded over 10 times for them to understand the process and the documentation I had obtained.

On the day of the appointment, I had to take Max in around 7:00 in the morning. I was totally nervous and scared about him going under. They were going to have to put a needle in his arm.

It was May 8, 2015, and he went in the back crying. The entire process lasted about one hour. They monitored his vitals while under and would come to the waiting room about every 10 to 15 minutes to update me. When they were finished, I had to go in the back. He was still under heavy sedation. The nurse gave me tips about what to expect when we got home.

I carried him to the car and strapped him into the car seat. I could barely drive the two minutes around the corner to our house because I was so concerned about how sedated he was. He wasn't able to control his neck and head very well.

I took him home and inside to the couch because the nurse had said to keep him lying down for a few hours after the procedure. Once the sedation wore off completely though, Max was up and running and jumping like nothing had happened. He never complained about his mouth or his teeth hurting at all. I was scared because I thought that he could easily get hurt from falling, but he had no side effects from the sedation.

Max has since returned to the dentist twice for annual cleanings. The last appointment went very well. He was able to go back on his own, followed the dentist and hygienist's directions for the exam, and did minimal crying during the process.

Chapter 9

SUMMER SCHOOL

During my 2015 journey to get Max evaluated for early intervention, I failed at a lot of other things in life.

I was not a very good mother, wife, or teacher during this time. I was most definitely suffering.

The stress of the situation took its toll on my health and my relationships. Because of how much time and energy I was putting into getting help for my son, I didn't go to social events or hang out with friends. I stopped going to Mommy and Me classes. I stopped shopping or going out for coffee. I didn't have the energy to give anything to myself.

I am so thankful today for my husband and my few close friends that didn't give up on me or leave. They waited very patiently for me to grow, which I am still working on now.

The early intervention system couldn't give me all the help I needed. There was no community support outside school—heck, there was very little support and communication in school.

If I hadn't insistently asked questions, I wouldn't have learned most of the things I know now.

We made it through those six months of dealing with cancer, finding a developmental pediatrician, having multiple assessments done, finding private therapy, and getting major dental work done.

During these months, I was also trying to find summer work. As a teacher, I was still on 10-month pay. So, summer was coming, and I didn't have a summer job to pay for necessities. I was freaking out and getting nervous. Finally, I got a call from a high school in North County about summer school.

Intertwined with all of this was that Max would be out of school and we couldn't find a summer camp anywhere that would take him. Max was three with special needs, limited language, and no diagnosis. He was not fully potty-trained (he was going number two in a Pull-Up or diaper, but he knew when he had to go and would ask for the diaper to be put on and taken off when he was done).

There was no summer camp that took children as young as three with special needs.

So, during all the appointments and therapy and changes to school, my husband, mother-in-law, and a few other immediate family members were still in denial about what I was telling them regarding Max. By the time we started speech therapy all the way in South Tampa, I knew what we were working with.

I had known it when the developmental pediatrician had said to do therapy and then come back for autism testing. I worked to tell my family that I believed he had autism and that it wasn't just a sensory processing thing or a natural speech delay that he would grow out of.

All of this is relevant because I was searching for a summer program that could handle his needs and they were thinking I could and should get him in anywhere. I felt defeated because I couldn't find a solution other than day care.

So, I ended up signing Max up for a day care. My husband insisted that Max go to school because his family thought that if he was around more children and socializing more with preschool teachers and students then he would talk or get better. The only place that I could find was recommended by my daughter's day care because they were affiliated.

Since I wasn't going to make enough money over summer school to cover all the expenses, I knew that I would need our savings to cover day care costs and more. My husband said that I shouldn't work. I didn't see how his logic about the cost of working summer school over the cost of staying at home made financial sense, but I was a mess. I tried to work it out and follow his suggestions, but to me, with the medical bills that were piling up and everyone's demands on me to keep Max in school, I couldn't think straight. So, I ended up taking the kids to school and not working. My husband wanted me to work on his business, trying to get additional contacts and contracts.

After the first two weeks, I knew the day care was not helping and, in fact, Max was learning all kinds of ways to manipulate the teachers without having to use language. The place was nice and took good care of him, but they weren't equipped to help him develop language or social skills.

I decided to take Social out of day care because she would start at a new school for the next school year and I didn't want to drive from one end of the county to the next every day, twice a day.

So, I had some one-on-one time with Social over the first month of summer. Then, I decided to take Max out of his day-care program because of the costs associated, time that I wanted to spend with him, and negative traits and behaviors that I could see him developing.

This really made my husband angry because he thought Max needed to be around other kids. Plus,

Pierce was already fuming hot with anger at me because of our lack of money and our having to use tax-return savings dollars to live for the summer.

I spent every day taking the kids to different activities. It was fun and busy. I was in great shape running after two kids that summer. We went to parks, playgrounds, children's museums, the zoo, and even spent three days in Orlando for SeaWorld. We also continued with Max's therapy and worked at home on his skills. We loved doing arts and crafts; the best was making bead bracelets.

During the summer and into the next school year, I had to spend hours on the phone with the insurance company. Max was getting a lot of speech and OT privately, and we also had to pay for the dental work. At the time, we had a $1,500 deductible per person on our insurance policy.

After you paid the deductible, then you had to pay 20 percent of the cost of the visit. Insurance companies suck because they really don't want to pay claims. In fact, I'm pretty sure they find ways to deny claims and not notify the provider or the patient until way later when you get a bill for the total amount from the provider. It's a special insurance lingo that you have to learn in order to get help.

I called every day. I cried, I screamed, I cussed people out, but I never stopped fighting the insurance company to pay the claim. I had to do this for years, and it got way worse before it got better.

Before we knew it, summer was over and back to school we all went. That summer was especially difficult on my marriage because of the expectations my husband had on me as his wife.

While we were transitioning Max into the public preschool setting and getting him help, I didn't like my husband's attitude. He seemed to be in denial, and his feelings toward me at that time made it difficult for us to find neutral ground to discuss what to do next to help Max. I felt alone in everything that I did, but I also thought that I needed Pierce's approval and thoughts about what to do.

Most often, we would just end up in arguments over how I wasn't meeting my husband's needs.

There is no way to explain how much time and energy I put into finding answers for my son. It became everything I did and everything I thought about. I couldn't sleep at night, and I had those days and nights where I felt inadequate to be his mother.

How can you give and take care of so many others when you hardly take care of yourself? It's impossible.

This only escalated the tension in our marriage.

Chapter 10

MAJOR PROBLEMS

At the end of the summer, we spent several weeks looking into private schools again. We went to two interviews at two different schools.

Both schools said that we would have to provide an aide for my son.

So, I was to pay their weekly tuition plus the cost of the aide for the class.

We were looking at private schools because, in our opinion, even though things had improved, the public school had not met its end of the agreement. At this point, I knew that Max needed to be in public school but also that I would have to spend time and dollars on as much private therapy as possible to get him the help he needed. So, Max went back to the public elementary school in Ms. Kennedy's class in August 2015.

Major problems would unfold over the next few months, but the first week went well. In fact, I laugh now when I open the planner and see the first week filled with smiling green faces.

Ms. Kennedy's comments were:

"Max had a very good day!"

"Max is doing a great job at following one-step directions. He does not want me to be out of his sight. ☺"

"Max ate a good breakfast. He didn't want to eat his sandwich at lunch. I filled his cup with water this morning. ☺"

"Happy weekend!"

Then week two started, and the honeymoon was over.

I knew in the second week that the teacher and the assistant, Ms. Kay, didn't have adequate training on how to work with children with special needs like my son.

Though my son had spectrum behavior, we hadn't had him diagnosed yet because the professional medical opinion had been to wait a year and do therapy. Though we'd had a rough start during the first six months of Max's initial school experience, my husband and I determined that we would do better at communicating with our son's teachers this time.

We talked to Ms. Kennedy prior to school starting and were clear about his needs and what worked best with him. However, during the second week, a permission form for a weighted vest was sent home. Weighted vests can help students with autism or other special needs by helping to provide the deep sensory input they seek that can often keep them from focusing. The concern is that without proper supervision weighted vests or blankets can pose a safety concern; especially with children that are nonverbal.

On the seventh day of school, the teacher wrote:

"Max has OT in class on Mondays. On Wednesdays, OT is a pullout. [Pullout means to be removed from a class for one-on-one therapy.] Speech is on Mondays and Wednesdays. Max does not want to transition from me. He will not work with my assistant. Max will cry and run if I walk away. The speech therapist was bringing Max with her to work in another room with other children in speech. Max will hit and kick at me or other objects. He does this when I make him comply with directions. We are working on following class expectations. Ms. Kay is working very hard to build a relationship with Max."

She gave all that detail about therapy because I had asked on Monday for information about transitions, the therapy schedule, and difficult behaviors. I explained that we had a calendar and would make sure that we continued to talk to Max about school to help make his next day better.

I tried to be very nice and reassuring during week two because I could tell that Ms. Kay was already becoming very frustrated and annoyed by his behavior and transitions. I suggested that she reassure him that it was safe to leave with the other teachers.

In our house, we thought it was odd that she was writing and saying that Max was being so clingy because we hadn't experienced that before—it was a new behavior. We weren't sure what was going on, and when I asked if I should come observe his transitions, she said it wasn't necessary.

In week two, Max wet his pants at PE, closed his finger in the door, ran out of speech therapy, and climbed on the classroom furniture.

On Thursday of week two, Ms. Kennedy wrote:

"Max is trying to climb everywhere. He wants to run around the room. If you can, please send the forms back regarding the weighted vest and blanket. Thank you."

I had already gone through the weighted vest request the previous year and had declined. So, I told her that we didn't want any weighted materials used with our son. Then, she sent the weighted blanket and vest request home again. My response was:

"We are not comfortable at this time with using the weighted vest. We did not see significant changes when we tried it in private therapy. We would like to give him more time to transition and learn your rules, expectations, and schedule. We are continuing to talk and work at home. Please continue to provide your suggestions and observations. We appreciate your knowledge."

The teacher and I had a conference call on September 18. She did most of the talking, complaining about his behavior. All of my suggestions to visit, observe, and follow tips that had worked in the past were dismissed. She clearly didn't want to talk about solutions; she wanted to complain to me.

After listening to her for almost 30 minutes, I finally spoke freely. She was talking about school and great teachers, and I responded that none of this was about great teachers or schools and that everything was about my son and his needs. That deeply upset her and she went cold and wouldn't talk anymore

What she didn't understand was that I was already aware as a parent what struggles my child would have to face. We reached a place where we knew that our views and ideas were on opposite ends.

After this call, things began to decline. Each week, incidents increased in terms of dangerous or atypical behavior. Things were happening that had *never* happened before. I couldn't explain them.

Max suddenly was wetting the cot at naptime. He was hitting the teacher's assistant, running away or out of the classroom, pulling down his pants, urinating on the class rug, refusing to go with Grandma at pick-up, running around in the cafeteria, and running out of the classroom.

The problems got to the point where he wasn't safe at school.

I was having a very hard time sleeping because I was having dreams of him running out of the school, toward our home, and no one noticing or catching him before he was injured.

As the weeks progressed and problems escalated, Max ran from the OT and speech therapists in mid-December. He ran all the way to the front of the school and up the stairs to the media center. The school principal had to chase him down!

Now they asked for a meeting. I couldn't sleep, and we were about to go on winter vacation.

Working with Ms. Kennedy was very difficult, and she felt it appropriate to tell me that Max would qualify for the autism spectrum disorder program at a different school. She was sure he would meet all the criteria.

I found out that she was telling other teachers that she believed my son didn't belong at the school. I always tried to respond accurately and politely but knew that she had issues with my child. At pick-up, she always provided negative feedback, and my husband had to tell her not to share information with anyone but us.

As the problems increased, I became uneasy about sending Max to school. In the second week of January, I was able to get a meeting with everyone, including the principal and my parent advocate. A parent advocate is someone who knows the laws regarding education and accommodations for special education students. Our advocate was provided for free by the district. I learned about this free service from a friend that I work with. I had gone to talk with her because I wanted more help with working with the school and the IEP team, and she recommended a specific advocate that she had used for her son.

Chapter 11

HOT LUNCH

Prior to the January meeting, we decided that we wanted Max moved out of the classroom.

I immediately requested a meeting with the principal regarding a teacher change. I had to explain all the times we talked on the phone, in person, or through email.

At this time, as new as I was to the IEP/ESE world, I had not taken notes about what the teacher had said in those calls. That's where situations can easily become he said/she said.

The principal wanted to know why we hadn't come to him before, and we explained how the behavior had significantly increased and that, at this point, it was a safety concern. The teacher was not physically able to run or chase after my son.

In the previous school year, Max had not had any of these severe behaviors.

My gut was telling me that my nonverbal child was trying to communicate with me that something was wrong.

We met with the principal and he wanted to wait until the January meeting to decide what to do. I had already talked to Ms. Miller and Ms. Rosalyn about whether they would take him back and they had both agreed. It was actually Ms. Rosalyn who spoke up about how Ms. Kennedy was talking about and to Max at school. Ms. Rosalyn went to Ms. Miller and had her call me. If it hadn't been for Ms. Rosalyn taking a stand for what was right, then my son could have continued to stay in a terrible learning environment that was causing him to academically decline.

At the meeting related to my teacher change request, we were told that Max would try to leave the classroom over 30 times within a three- to four-hour day! His GOLD performance scores went down, which is an observation-based assessment that measures the skills of preschool students. His performance and behavior were worsening on all levels. None of this was what we had been working on for months, and we hadn't previously experienced any of these things with our child.

As the meeting progressed, I continued to ask the

same question: "When will Max be moved out of this classroom?"

At the end of the meeting, the principal still wouldn't make a decision. He said he needed to talk to the other teachers.

Later that day, he called and informed us that Max would be moved into the old class with Ms. Miller and Ms. Rosalyn. The meeting was Monday, and Max's first day in the class was Wednesday.

On Thursday, I got a call at work in the middle of the day—Ms. Miller was calling, and she seemed really mad. She started asking me about Max's lunch and whether he was supposed to eat in the cafeteria. She laid into me, telling me that he was lying down on his cot looking hungry, and she informed me that I was not packing an appropriate lunch for my child.

I told her that he got free lunch and that I had packed a snack as I had been directed to do during school orientation.

She said, "OH!", and her entire demeanor completely changed on the phone.

Then there was a long pause. She said, "Ruth, I don't think he's been getting a lunch! They haven't been taking him to the cafeteria, and they told me that he packs his lunch and that is what he is supposed to eat."

My mouth dropped open in shock. "*Oh my God*. Are you telling me that they haven't been giving him his free hot lunch?!"

She said, "I don't think so."

We continued to talk, and I tried to stay calm. We decided it was best to contact the school cafeteria manager and request a copy of Max's transactions and records just to verify our suspicions.

I called the cafeteria manager and gave her all the information. I explained that I believed that my child was not being taken to the cafeteria for lunch and that he hadn't been able to access his free lunch.

"Oh no!" she said. "Okay, let's pull up his file."

We went over his file, and she could see that he had gotten free breakfast every day.

Then she could see that there was $10 on his account from the beginning of the school year and that our application had been approved for reduced lunch (which was free in our Title I elementary school).

She could see that Max had received the lunch up until September 17, then lunch had stopped.

She could see that there were a few dates in December that he had received a lunch but, other than that, he hadn't been coming to the cafeteria to receive the food. She explained that the student had to be present and seen in order to get the lunch.

I told her that I needed a copy of the document emailed to me and also needed a copy to go to the principal. She said, "Okay."

I then hung up the phone and went back to work a hot mess. I waited for the next break and called the school. I told the secretary who I was and that I was calling because I needed to see the principal immediately that day.

She already knew.

The cafeteria manager had been so kind and apologetic throughout the conversation but hadn't been able to explain why Max wasn't being served.

I was able to let the principal know that I would be there right away to meet. Then I had to call my husband and try to explain through my anger, fear, and tears. We both went to speak to the principal.

When going to speak with the principal, I was an emotional wreck and my husband was Mr. Twenty Questions with a side of legal attitude.

The principal asked if I wanted to talk to the teacher about it and that he could have her come down.

I was so furious about my son not having lunch for four months that there was no way I wanted to see or talk to the woman. In addition, my son had been removed from her class due to his behavior. Now, just three days into the new classroom, the behaviors were nonexistent.

I told the principal that my son had been acting up because it was the only way he could communicate that the teacher wasn't treating him right and she had, in fact, been denying him his free hot lunch every day for four months.

What would have happened if I hadn't fought to get my child removed from her class? How many months would Max have gone without lunch then?

After a long meeting, we left, and the principal didn't seem concerned about the legal concerns we had brought to his attention. He was not acting like he was going to be on the case at all.

Now that my son was out of the room, the attitude seemed to be that none of the teacher's actions could be changed or altered. My son was now getting his hot lunch every day and was away from the teacher.

I went home and was so pissed off that I needed to do something. It was apparent that the principal wasn't going to do anything.

So, I called and reported the teacher to the Department of Children and Families (DCF). This action caused the district to open an Office of Professional Standards investigation (OPS).

Since I had a sinking feeling in my stomach that the teacher was going to go without warning or discipline and could then do this to another student, I had to act at the highest level. My son was now safe and not subject to her care, but what she had done was terrible.

The DCF went to the school and interviewed the teachers and principal. Then the district OPS also had to investigate.

No one followed up with us, the parents. No one contacted us to get our story, and no one asked what information we had about our records that indicated Max had not received lunch. I had the letter about receiving reduced lunch, the check and account balance of $10 from the deposit I'd sent at the beginning of the year, the planner with notes about lunch, and my story about how the teacher had known he needed a lunch. No one asked for our side of the story.

We had had conversations about Max needing to eat with his peers and try new foods in his lunch. If he didn't eat everything, it was okay, but I wanted him to try. I had been sending the same snack all school year—cheese, apple, and popcorn. In the beginning of the year (about the first 10 days), I had even sent a second bagged lunch because we hadn't received the notice about free lunch yet. Even though Max had the credit on his account and was getting a lunch sent from home the first 10 days of school, the school had records that he had been taken to the cafeteria and had gotten a free lunch for the first three to four weeks of school.

Once we received the letter about the reduced or free lunch credit, I stopped sending the second bag. The teacher gave me the lunch letter. Then, in September, immediately after our phone conversation, the teacher stopped taking him to lunch.

When weeks went by with no follow-up, we decided to follow up ourselves. We contacted the district and talked to the investigator. I talked to him on the phone and requested a meeting.

During this time, we had a conversation regarding my concerns and why I hadn't been interviewed or why a follow-up regarding the investigation hadn't been provided to the parents.

The detective was very rude when I continued to ask him about who I could talk to in order to schedule a meeting. He got really impatient and condescending with me and said that he didn't know and was sure I could find out since I worked for the district.

I'm a district employee, and my husband is a former employee. We have seen OPS in action with teachers and how they take the parents' side of the situation every time and the teacher gets a letter or is disciplined. This time, it seemed completely the opposite.

It was rude to call me out as an employee because I had never used my knowledge or position to file complaints as a parent.

I clarified really quickly that I was making a complaint as a parent and not as an employee and that it was not okay to bring that up in our conversations. I expected to be treated as a parent, and I expected to be provided with the requested information to make an appointment. He was trying to make it very difficult to get additional information. He wouldn't talk on the phone, and he refused to give me the phone number and name to make the appointment myself.

I called my husband after my long, drawn-out conversation with the rude investigator because I was kind of shocked that he had treated me the way he had. So, my husband called him too. We were finally able to schedule a time to meet with the detective.

When we went to the detective's office, I took all my documents as evidence of what my claims were, but he never asked for any of it. He asked us what we wanted—we both said answers.

He couldn't give us any answers.

All he could tell us was that our child hadn't gone hungry, that I had been providing a lunch (the snack I sent every day as directed by the teacher at open house procedures), the school had been providing a snack, and the teacher and the principal were supporting each other. No one would or could answer why Max had stopped receiving a lunch.

We told the detective that we believed the teacher had withheld our son from the cafeteria as a form of punishment.

I even went to the pediatrician's office to have his weight and health checked. Since he would eat when he got home, he didn't have any weight loss, so he wasn't "being neglected."

We discussed that our child has special needs, is nonverbal, and that the teacher was punishing him. She had never asked for us to send a lunch, and she had never complained about lunchroom behavior. She'd lied when interviewed, and the principal had backed her up and told interviewers that a snack had been provided by the school. No other preschool classroom had a snack provided by the school.

Remember, my son had been in the other preschool class the previous year and was now back in that classroom. They didn't get a school snack. No notes or requests for a snack had been sent home, and the teacher and principal supported that statement.

Everyone was asking what we wanted.

We had to keep repeating that the teacher needed to be disciplined and removed from the classroom so that she couldn't hurt another child.

During this time, I also researched the woman's teaching certificate and found out that she wasn't certified in special education.

Therefore, she had no training in how to be a case manager for a child with an IEP. She was not qualified to work with special needs children, and she needed to be removed from that environment.

None of that happened, and she continued to be in the same classroom with the same lack of qualifications.

To my knowledge, no reprimand was given because the findings were unsubstantiated. She claimed it was a communication problem and pleaded a misunderstanding on her part. So, she totally and completely lied because I told her to her face that my son was to get lunch.

She looked at the letter for free and reduced lunch in the parking lot and saw that he was to receive it. We talked on the phone, and I said I wanted him to get the lunch because it was free. And yet, she lied and claimed a misunderstanding and continued to work with children.

To the school, my son was out of her class, so what more did I want? They didn't understand that this was about more than my child at this point.

I learned a lot about myself and what you need to fight the district—a big, expensive special needs lawyer.

You can't go into the fight without a big dog to call out the lies and give your child the answers he deserves for how wrongfully he was treated.

From this moment forward, my life forever changed.

I realized just how poor we were and how much we were relying on the school to care for and help our son. We couldn't afford the $300 legal fee to see if we had a case against the district. We had to keep fighting.

When I share what happened to my son, people's mouths hang open, and they ask, "How is that possible?"

Sadly, almost all parents with children on the spectrum have a story to tell about how their child was mistreated. It's very sad that, within the education system, children with special needs that have limited language are so often victims of mistreatment.

Chapter 12

MOVING ON

Once the fight with the school and school district started, and my son had been in an abusive classroom environment for half the school year, my outlook on my job, parenthood, and life changed.

I lost that fight, but what could I learn from it that would help me protect and educate my child safely, as well as improve special education programs for other kids like Max?

I still had trouble sleeping, as well as difficulty continuing to work for the same system that had allowed my son to be mistreated. The only thing that helped me was finding solutions and access to therapy that would help my son. I kept pushing to find services and resources.

We had recently started going to We Rock the Spectrum for my son to play with the OT equipment in the gym. I had procrastinated about going because I'd thought it was too much money to get in. I finally broke down and tossed my money at the daily admittance for two kids—$22. It was awesome! Not only was it a place that other people understood my son, but it was great for me too. There were lots of toys and sensory-friendly swings and slides, a trampoline, and even a zip line. The best part was that the owner provided endless opportunities for therapy, guest lectures, and recommendations.

At this point, Max was still without a medical diagnosis because the pediatrician had said to wait. Ironically, as my son was jumping on the trampoline, the gym owner recommended applied behavior analysis (ABA) therapy to us and specifically mentioned one of my very good friends for the therapy. I was immediately optimistic—ABA is the number-one recommended therapy for children with autism.

I called and talked to that friend about the gym, ABA, and my son. She was like a huge hug of reassurance and support.

I decided that we would try ABA to see if it would help my son. I signed him up for the social skills class at the gym, which was based on ABA. I also called and made another appointment to see the developmental pediatrician. We started going to the gym at the end of

2015 and started social skills class in January 2016, finishing our first eight-week session on March 8.

I knew within the first four weeks at social skills class that it was working even though it was only one hour a week, and the beginning was rough. Max couldn't sit cross-legged. I didn't even know that he didn't have that ability or strength in his core. So, we added that to his OT program.

If I could get an autism spectrum disorder (ASD) diagnosis, then I could get more money, grants, and services for Max. The ASD diagnosis would open up access and opportunities. We made an appointment to go back to USF on March 14.

Pierce and I went to the appointment and were told that there had been a scheduling error and that we would not be able to get a diagnosis that day because the doctor didn't have enough time to do the necessary screening and testing. We were sad and must have looked it.

The doctor asked us why we wanted the autism testing done now. I shared with her that I knew we needed the medical diagnosis for insurance—that I was at a place where I couldn't help my son anymore because I lacked a medical diagnosis. The insurance would only cover speech and OT, no ABA therapy. I had my binder of IEP documents, speech evaluations, OT evaluations, and the documents from social skills class.

She looked at the binder, and we went over the documents from the other specialists. She had not heard of the social skills class and asked about that too.

She decided to help us that day.

The doctor decided after observing Max, reading the reports, and talking to us that she could move forward with giving us the ASD diagnosis. She had me take many, many packets of evaluation questionnaires for his teachers and us to fill out.

The teacher was very helpful in getting the paperwork done and was supportive and collaborative with the process. Once complete, we mailed them back to the doctor. Within a few weeks, I had the official reports that needed to be submitted to the insurance company in order to request ABA therapy.

I thought that getting the medical diagnosis would be like waving a magic wand to get the services I needed for my son. Well, it was true, but it also wasn't.

I had to fight and fight with the insurance company. I had to get medical necessity letters from my pediatrician as well as spend hours on the phone with the insurance company. Trying to get the insurance company to cover services, pay services, or deal with documents for the flexible spending accounts was truly a nightmare and pretty much a part-time job.

It's hard to tell the entire story or create a full picture of all the moving pieces that were happening at the same time.

Throughout our marriage, Pierce and I had been renting a two-bedroom apartment while his parents had been living in the house he'd grown up in. As time went by, the house became too much for his parents to maintain and manage, so he made a deal with them. If they let us move in, then he would be responsible for property updates and pay rent for the house. They moved into an apartment, and he started to renovate the house so that our family of four could live there. Pierce had to fully renovate the inside of the house and do major yard work on the overgrown property. In exchange, we knew would have a safe place for our family.

From January to the end of March, my husband was gone most of the time. He was working on his business and completely renovating his parents' house for those three months. He would pick up our son and take him to the house to play and work. Then Pierce would go back to work on the house. He did almost all the work completely by himself. Our lease was up at the end of March, and we had to move into the house.

During these times when Pierce had work, his business and then renovating the house, my mom would spend a lot of time on the weekends coming to visit Max. She would be there to listen and help with the kids while I tried to do laundry. Max loved her so much. He could never tell her but he would always get a huge smile on his face when she would visit. He would climb on her and she would give him lots of nana kisses. My mom was really my go to person when I needed to vent my frustrations. She would often text or call to check on me and Max in between visits.

When we moved into the house, it still didn't have a kitchen. We had a completed bathroom and one other bathroom that was still being finished, but the biggest issue was the cabinets. They had been ordered a month prior but had had at least three reschedules or delays on their arrival. Without the cabinets, we couldn't have counters or appliances. So, for about the first month of moving into the new house, I cooked in the dining room with a microwave, Crock-Pot, and rice cooker. Then I signed us up for meals to be delivered twice a week to try to break up the same meals of chicken and rice.

After I cooked, I would have to wash the dishes in the bathtub.

After all the times I'd cried in the kitchen of our tiny apartment because we needed more space, an actual working dishwasher, a washing machine and dryer that didn't require a full day on the weekend to drag the kids and clothes to the laundry room, a backyard for the kids to play, and a place to store all the business stuff—it had happened. We had all those things or would have them soon.

Chapter 13

FINANCIAL HARDSHIP

It seemed like the autism diagnostic process was fast and easy, which led me to think that things would change immediately, but it was, in fact, still a continued struggle.

We were in the social skills class at We Rock the Spectrum and going to the speech therapy and OT in Tampa, as well as keeping Max in the public blended preschool. During this time, we were able to get the diagnosis of ASD and move forward to get ABA therapy for the summer.

All of this came with heavy financial hardship, especially for myself. My husband was working a part-time job and running his business to make money to live and renovate the house. I was taking on the full financial responsibility of all of Max's therapy, doctors' appointments, and insurance billing. We had other financial problems because we had debt that we couldn't pay on. Max's social skills class was $40 per session, once a week. Speech therapy was a $40 to $50 out-of-pocket expense for every 30-minute session. OT was around $80 to $90 for every 30 minutes. Those expenses were if the insurance company processed and paid the claim. Looking at ABA therapy, the out-of-pocket costs would be approximately $100 to $120 per hour after insurance adjusted the rate. At the time, my insurance individual out-of- pocket maximum was $4,000. So, my responsibility for the year was an additional $4,000, but I was already struggling with regular bills.

As the summer of 2016 approached, we were planning to have ABA therapy in our home for at least half a day, four to five days a week. We had the in-home evaluation done, and I thought everything was ready to go.

I talked to the director and a big change happened for them—suddenly, they weren't going to be able to provide in-home therapy. My summer plans were gone, and I was left scrambling to find a place for Max to go for the summer. I knew that the day care from last summer was out of the question. Finally, I found an autism summer camp. It would cost $110 to $145 a week, and I would need someone to drop him off in the morning. My mother-in-law stepped up to help drop Max off four days a week. Her health had improved—

she was cancer free and had recovered from her surgery and treatments.

Then I had to pay for Social to continue to go to school during the summer. I had a part-time job set up, but I knew that with the $165 a week for my daughter and the money for my son, there wasn't going to be enough to pay all the bills and still eat.

I had to stop taking Max to speech and OT therapy over the summer because I would need to find a second afternoon job. I couldn't afford to miss work in order to drive him, and then there was the gas and toll money, on top of the therapy bill.

Everyone wanted money that summer, and I struggled to keep up with the payments. I did everything I could think of to make money or save money. I had already given up shopping for new clothes or shoes. I didn't cut my hair or pay for any grooming. I went to the Salvation Army on Wednesdays (because everything is half price) to buy summer shorts for the kids and myself. I checked free boards and picked up toys, clothes, and even food.

I had no credit, and we were working on filing for bankruptcy. I sold Mary Kay, I asked for money, I did a jam berry fundraiser, and I sold anything I could. I worked a summer teaching job and used Care.com to find a family that needed their teens tutored in the afternoons.

This time of absolutely no money, being behind on bills, not having any credit, and working my butt off to try to live made me research financial aid and find grants. I realized that I wasn't poor enough to get real help, but I didn't have money to access the services I needed for my child.

The summer at the autism camp was great for Max. The staff really knew what he needed and the class fit his needs, so he could continue to practice and learn school skills. During the summer, I got a letter of medical necessity for the insurance company from my pediatrician to seek all the therapy Max needed. I was also able to find the Early Autism Intervention Clinic. I laugh at myself when I think back to that day when I went into the office and just stood there.

I said, "I have an ASD diagnosis and insurance, and I want information to get my son ABA therapy."

I stood there, rooted, because I needed help, and I wasn't going to leave without paperwork. The doctor came out and suggested I bring Max in to visit him. We went in and talked and started the process. I didn't really know that we were starting a different type of ABA because I was so new to autism and treatments at the time.

Meeting with the doctor was amazing for me. He was able to get in contact with a person at my insurance company—a direct extension contact! That was unheard of and damn near impossible.

I remember telling my husband about that and how it had been worth paying for the therapy just for the case manager and direct contact with our insurance company. Working with the clinic started to make my duties fewer and easier.

While all this was changing and developing, I was still preparing grant paperwork and working two jobs to try to make ends meet and keep us fed. We received a $2,000 medical grant from United Healthcare Children's Foundation to cover the cost of the ABA, as well as speech and OT. The grant helped give me that push to start getting Max into ABA therapy at the clinic. We also resumed OT and speech once I went back to work teaching full-time. Receiving this grant was the most amazing feeling. I really felt like a burden was lifting and I could push to get Max more help. The guilt of not knowing how to provide necessities for my family was overwhelming, and this grant helped to ease my financial pain.

During the summer, my mom stopped talking to me. She had spent a lot of time with us up until that point, listening to me vent about the stress I felt with work, marriage, life, finances, and the kids.

I'm not certain why she stopped talking, texting, or visiting with us but she completely cut communication for almost a year. My grandma would call and tell me to call her; she would tell me, and apparently my mom, that we needed to stop being stubborn and talk with each other.

I'm not sure if I did something that upset her or if she didn't like the situation I was in with my family at the time. The combination of financial stress, marital stress, and the constant activity of finding help for Max was pretty overwhelming. I had busied myself so much with the day-to-day work, phone calls, appointments, and daily chores of life to the point that I had no outside personal life. So, when my mom just stopped talking to me, it was very difficult. She had been a listening ear, shoulder to cry on, and coach through all the tears.

One of the worst parts was that being cut off definitely brought back old feelings and memories of being abandoned. Those were issues that I thought I'd dealt with but obviously hadn't—not completely. After my mom moved back to Florida, back in my college days, she lived on her own for a while before ending up with a new boyfriend. She did all kinds of things that I never expected from her, like piercing her body and getting tattoos, and ended up remarrying. We didn't talk or spend much time together at that point because she was with her new husband. Then, after almost a decade of separation, she became much more involved when I got married and had children.

So, obviously, when she stopped talking to me, it was very hurtful.

My aunt Debbie, her only sister and living sibling, died in February 2017. That was the first time I saw my mother since the spring of 2016. It wasn't a good time to see her, given the circumstances, but I think that it did help start to bring some communication back.

I know that she'll never tell me why she stopped talking to me during that summer, and I have to decide how I'll move forward dealing with her and my family.

My son loves her so much. He cannot find those words to tell her but he still gets a big smile any time he sees her. I want her to be in his life, but I don't want my children to have a hit and miss relationship with her. I want them to see her consistently, even if it's just on holidays and birthdays.

Chapter 14

MARRIAGE

Throughout the journey of finding my son his therapy and diagnosis, I was most certain that I would end up divorced. We went through a time when my husband told me regularly that he wanted a divorce and wasn't happy. It was exhausting because I felt alone in life and alone in trying to help my son. When I think back, it seems like Pierce and I were going in opposite directions, and nothing he said to me made it better or less painful. I was struggling in all parts of my life and taking all things personally. It was like everything was my fault and blamed on me, but yet there was nothing I could do to fix it. The most devastating feeling is that something is broken and there is nothing you can do about it. During this time, my husband's only answer was divorce—that was his way to fix it.

The divorce conversations started about six months into my second pregnancy (2013) and didn't stop until about the end of 2015 or beginning of 2016.

I cried and stressed over how I would make it if Pierce left. It was difficult enough dealing with my son's behavior, and the rest of my life was a mess. I would cry at work, in my kitchen, in the shower, in the car. I had feelings of not being good enough and that I would never be enough for anyone. The only thing I could do, day in and day out, was continue to learn about my children and provide for them. I would research and make appointments for Max. I tried to focus on business and work, but it was very challenging.

It's borderline insanity to work side-by-side with your husband on a business he created while he is so upset with you and often telling you he wants a divorce to solve the problem. But I kept working and learning.

I was so sad during this time that I would sometimes just fall apart over one phrase from my husband. I took the things he told me so personally and dwelled on the hurtful things he said, over and over.

When he was in a good mood, we would have normal conversations about our day at work or with the kids, and he would be more helpful with tasks around the house.

I tried to do things that I thought would make him happy but which were totally outside of my understanding or knowledge. I wanted to make him happy because when he was upset, he would lecture me for hours. He would talk about all the things I wasn't doing to help him and how upsetting it was that I wasn't doing what he needed. He would bring up the same events or occasions over and over. I remember thinking that it was like a form of torture to have to listen for hours, barely being able to hold a conversation because when I did try to explain or talk, it only escalated the situation. He would bring up the same events or occasions over and over, and arguing with him was like a long marathon of being out-talked. I was already so sleep-deprived and exhausted that staying up extra hours took its toll.

One day, I decided that it didn't matter anymore if my husband wanted a divorce—he could have one. I no longer had the energy to go to marriage counseling on my own, to fight or argue with him, or to try to convince him I was worth staying for. If he was that unhappy, then he needed to leave. I would find a way to be okay. Many, many other women had figured it out and still managed to care for their families. If I could get my son help, that was the most important thing at the time.

Divorce rates are significantly higher in families with children with special needs. It is very difficult for two people to be on the same page in dealing with autism or special needs. Most often, denial is the biggest problem, and we went through a lot of denial in both of our families. Many times, people are not willing to be patient in waiting for another person to accept a diagnosis. Other times, a person is not willing to accept a way of life, treatment, or therapy.

Throughout the arguments and contemplations of divorce, I knew that divorce wasn't what either of us really wanted. It just took over two years to scream it into my brain and for Pierce to get tired enough to realize that we did want to work it out.

Our marriage and our family are working for us now.

My husband respects how much I worked to find opportunities for Max. He is an amazing father and the most supportive and encouraging husband today. He has been the first and biggest fan of my writing. It was Pierce who told me to share my posts about how I was able to get Max help. He was the one who made my first logo for my website and was the first person to encourage me to buy my domain name and share my articles and celebrate the views.

Everyone is being cared for, and we have our strength together. I'm proud to say that, right now, I do have it figured out. It's not perfect, and we have our battle wounds and scars, but we kept getting back up and stayed in the fight. I also understand that both Pierce and I are in a voluntary agreement that could be ended any day by either of us. Marriage is not easy or simple, and there is no answer on how to guarantee it will work. I thought for sure that my family would end in divorce a few years ago. Now, looking at us, I see the growth potential. I see how my children benefit from our communication, teamwork, and honesty.

There is a lot of sacrifice on our part to make our house run daily, and we try not to complain or place blame when the ball gets dropped. Living, working, playing, and raising children together is a huge task and, as people, my husband and I are complete opposites. It makes it challenging to get on the same page or even to agree to disagree. We have learned more about each other and each other's needs. Now, we, as husband and wife, can help our son so much more.

I am so thankful for the flexibility in my husband's schedule, and it is amazing to see him be a great father. My father didn't do the day-to-day interactions that my children get to experience, and I know that Pierce will have a major impact on their growth and development because he is so involved. Seeing the love that a child has for their father is beautiful, and the safety and protection he provides them makes them feel free to develop and experiment.

Pierce is there every morning keeping the schedule, better than I, might I say. I leave for work while everyone is sleeping and he is the best at making sure everyone is cared for; how many kids can say their dad cooks them a hot breakfast and walks them to school every day? That's pretty special. Some days, I wish I could see them walking to school together—it may seem like a regular thing, but it really is special. I have to leave early to get to work each day, so I'm never there when the kids leave for school.

Whether people stay married, never marry, or live a divorced life, there has to be a united front for the children. I see the moms without active husbands or dads being treated differently at school. The way that school administrators and personnel speak to them regarding their children's needs is not how my conversations, questions, or concerns go.

So, if you do not stay together in your relationship, remember to find a way to stay together on the care and treatment of your special needs child.

Chapter 15

PERMISSION

Max's first successful school year was the 2016-2017 year with Ms. Smith. This was the first time he was able to stay in the same school class for an entire school year—10 months. He had been at the school for two and a half years but had three teachers during the first year and a half.

We put Max in the blended program at his zoned public school. He had an IEP that would give him 30 minutes of OT and 60 minutes of speech therapy, as well as behavioral supports. Then, after school, four days a week, he would have ABA therapy and OT and speech. This was the first time that we had a complete package of services and care for our son. We had a program at school and a private therapy program.

My husband was nervous and skeptical at first, but our plan was to have Max attend the blended model four days a week, all day. On Tuesday and Thursday, after school, he would go to his ABA clinic for two hours of therapy. Then, on Friday, we wouldn't send him to public preschool but instead would send him to the ABA clinic for six hours that day. Monday would be his rest night, and on Wednesday we would drive to speech and OT in South Tampa.

We started school on August 16. Before school started, I went to observe the class he would enter. In May of the previous year, I visited and added suggestions to his IEP that would be more appropriate for voluntary prekindergarten (VPK) which is a free three and a half hours of school each day provided by state funding to prepare young kids for kindergarten. I was sure Max needed more support during center time and also some major transition support.

Once we were in the class in the beginning of the year, we contacted the parent advocate and requested a reevaluation. Max would need it in order to have his eligibility determined for kindergarten. It was decided that the developmental delay category would be dropped. We officially started the process in August and didn't have our final meeting until January.

As I read and experienced more of the ABA verbal behavior model, I could see where the public school model was falling short for my son, but the cost of full-time ABA therapy was beyond my financial ability. In fact, I could hardly afford 10 hours a week. In just one month, Max met his deductible of $1,500.

I do believe that the blended model is very good and that my son really needs to be with, play with, and learn with typical students. However, I also know that my son is substantially, maybe extremely, delayed in multiple categories. If I kept him in public school, how would he catch up in those areas that are so fundamental? We still wonder today how long it will take him to write or read at an age-appropriate level.

Through the learning and reading that I did, I realized how much more support my son needed in the traditional class. I requested a behavior plan, which is an additional document attached to the IEP that supports one of the IEP goals. So, we wanted to improve Max's behavior in this way so that he could be successful in achieving his learning goal.

We had three meetings with the IEP team, teacher, administrator, speech therapist, OT, behavior coach, and parent advocate. In the first meeting, I just about ripped up the behavior plan. It was confusing, not aligned to any of the goals, and it didn't have any data to support the behavior. We had no baseline to determine how we could improve and measure improvement. It was completely arbitrary.

After the first meeting, with the behavior plan fail, the behavior specialist was able to work with the teacher to collect data. The problem was the teacher was having a difficult time identifying the problem behavior. Together, after data was collected, we, as a team, were able to rewrite the goal and came up with strategies to keep Max on task.

The general issue was that, on an activity he didn't like, Max was unable to complete the task without excessive redirection or intervention. The suggestion was a type of token board that he could earn for positive behavior. When he completed the chart, then he got to choose a preferred activity. The teacher came up with a train and stamp system. She started with one to three train cars and Max had to earn a stamp on the train in order to be finished with the non-preferred activity and move to the preferred activity. She tested the strategies, and we had a third meeting.

At the third meeting, the teacher had data that showed the improvement of on-task behavior with the intervention. The parent advocate was very happy and pushed to adjust Max's IEP goals to align with his growth. The behavior plan did not become more aligned with ABA therapy or his ABA program, but it was proven to be successful when I forced the issue. If I hadn't demanded data, then the plan would have gone forward without any evidence or data.

I also asked the behavior specialist to assist the teacher because it's complicated to support and reflect or count the number of times you intervene within three to six minutes, all while still teaching the rest of the class. I knew as a teacher that the teacher needed support.

Overall, the experience of working with a teacher for a full year was successful for my child. The support and combination of the private therapy time was vital in that success. Without the evaluations and support from outside programs and professionals, I would have been without information, opinions, and data to guide my son's IEP meetings. I knew that it was working because I could observe the private therapy and even participate. However, public schools don't work that way. They are very closed off and don't involve parents.

At the last IEP of the year, the compliance person from the district complimented me on how prepared I always was for a meeting. I would take a lot of time each meeting to go over the goals and services. I would make sticky notes and bring other documents to support my questions and concerns. She told me that she appreciated my thoroughness and that so many other parents just show up and sign papers. She clearly appreciated me helping her do her job.

During the time that the IEP evaluation was being completed, I was struggling to get Max to therapy in South Tampa. It was wearing on me physically, but I continued to push.

I met my breaking point at the end of January.

Max had the flu and was throwing up for the two days prior to his therapy appointment. He had not gone to school that Wednesday but seemed well enough to go to therapy in the afternoon. I was not feeling well on that Wednesday in late January. I had a terrible stomachache. I thought it would be fine; I would just #momstrong this appointment. I would up my fluid intake and get him there. I could do it.

Well, I did it, but with a lot of throwing up in the parking lot that afternoon.

I felt so bad once I got to the appointment that I went outside to sit in my car against a tree. I started sweating and was concerned about the time. I got back to the car and had about 10 minutes before Max was done with therapy. I started getting sick and could barely make the plastic bag. I threw up all over my shoes and car. Then the office called because I wasn't inside!

I had to beg for them to bring Max out the back door because I was so sick. I was able to make it home in traffic but swore to never do that again.

Once I puked in the parking lot of the therapy center and had to deal with the center billing and insurance, I couldn't take anymore. I gave myself permission to stop taking my son to therapy. It was a low moment for me, realizing that I was physically not able to take Max while trying so hard for him. I needed a break, not just from going on Wednesdays, but from the paperwork, phone calls, and insurance problems.

I remember driving the car one day in November when the therapy office called to say I shouldn't come because my insurance would not pay the contracted rate.

I researched and called the insurance company—they claimed that a provider could not do what this provider was doing to us. They explained that they did pay and that if I noticed something didn't process, I should call and ask for it to be reprocessed. "It's the machine's fault," they said.

Then I talked to the provider and they gave me a totally different story about back pay, refusing to pay, and not paying the agreed amount. I didn't know whom to believe. The only truth I had was that my son was in need of help and it seemed like it was time to let speech and OT go at that point.

It was pretty liberating for me once I accepted that I wasn't failing. Instead, I celebrated and told our ABA case manager that I had finally given myself permission to stop. It feels like you are never doing enough to help your child and that there is always something that you can do better. That is an exhausting feeling and way to live. So, with some rest and time, we moved on.

That time allowed me to develop my blog, which I had tentatively started in Oct/Nov. 2016, and find swimming programs for Max. We thought that maybe it was time to find something fun to do after school instead of more school.

Chapter 16

MCKAY AND MOVING ON

The 2017 school year started in the summer for Max. The day after public school ended, he started at the private school full-time.

We have made a decision and commitment to try the verbal behavior model of applied behavior analysis (ABA) or (VB-ABA). Max attends school for six hours a day for one-on-one therapy from the same teacher all five days of the week.

Since I was able to get Max on the Children's Medical Services (CMS) insurance provided by the Florida State Health Department, they cover his ABA therapy. Once the school year starts, then I can also use the McKay Scholarship to pay for tuition. The therapy is working, and we are seeing changes in our son. Nevertheless, we still have battles to fight and lessons to learn on how to advocate for our child.

There is definitely a learning curve to the McKay Scholarship, and I do not recommend applying for it on your own. I don't understand how the state and county work together and get information. The lack of communication is a real issue.

When you have a problem, the state sends you directly to the county and they try to clean it up. We are currently having a big issue with my son's eligibility and information on the Florida state website. The school district was helpful in changing it, but the state didn't go back to update his eligibility score based on the corrected information.

The problem is that the website had my son's race as white and his eligibility as DD (developmentally delayed). My son at age five, going on six, cannot be classified as DD anymore because it is no longer a classification. All students have to be reevaluated and classified. I did that in January and he was eligible for ASD (autism spectrum disorder) and LI (language impaired).

My son is more than one race; he is black and white. However, the state website still has him classified as white. Race shouldn't be a big deal, but it is in our country. My son is fair, but he is still half black and has the right to be represented accurately on a state department of education website.

When you look into education, there is an emphasis on the achievement gap and equal access based on race. So, not only am I concerned about my child with autism, but I am also concerned with how he will be treated because of his race.

As we near the end of 2017, I am concerned that this will become a legal matter and that I will have to seek a lawyer to draft a letter requesting information and corrections to my son's file. My concern is that the matrix score is wrong and he should be the next score up, 253. This is important because the higher your matrix score, the more money you get in your scholarship. The matrix score is made up of five sections based on social, cognitive, communication and physical disabilities. Those sections are reflected in a student's IEP. The more services a student has the higher a student's score should be on that corresponding section. Then when all sections are added together the total score is calculated on a point scale. One point can mean the difference of almost $2,000 or more that the student's scholarship could be missing.

So, if we are to use McKay for the rest of his education, then think of the compounding numbers. Let's just say it was $2,000 each year; that's a total of $26,000 that will be denied to Max over the length of his education. But I don't know if the information is correct or incorrect because I can't get ahold of it.

For us, using the McKay Scholarship brought its own set of challenges and struggles that remain unsolved; we are thankful that we obtained the scholarship and could begin private school. Without private school, we would have struggled to make the major changes necessary to help Max begin to speak and learn.

Problems never really go away; they just change. However, some things do stay the same—like sedation dentistry again for my son in October 2017.

My son had a visit at the end of 2016 and it was perfect; no issues and no problem spots in his mouth. Then, six months later (at the end of May), he had a mouth full of problems. The biggest issues were that his two bottom teeth were not falling out, and he had a broken or fractured tooth in the back. I was so angry. We went from great to a disaster in six months. So, we had to schedule sessions to fix his teeth. We had an August appointment set for the sedation. It was estimated to cost us another $1,000 or more.

Well, August came and we had to reschedule because the office was under renovations that week. Then, we scheduled him for September 11. It's a terrible day to begin with, but it also happened to be the day that Hurricane Irma hit. I was on the phone with the office on Thursday and Friday, asking about what the office was going to do. They said to keep the appointment! They were crazy.

Well, on Saturday we were given emergency last-minute evacuation orders because the weather forecasters couldn't figure out where in the world this monster hurricane was going to land and what it would destroy in its path.

To make a long story short, there was no appointment on Monday. After a few weeks, we did get a makeup session in. My son had lost his two bottom teeth at that point, but it only saved me $80 in extraction fees. This time was more difficult for him.

He became angry as the medicine was wearing off because he thought he could move and control his body, but I was making him stay still or lie down. He was trying to move but couldn't control his limbs; he was out of control and not fun to deal with once we were home. I'm glad they were able to fix his teeth, but I never again want to deal with paying that much money or dealing with my child coming out of anesthesia.

Now, we will go to the dentist about three to four times a year to work more on prevention. We are also going to work on getting him to tolerate the dentist so that we don't have to deal with any more sedation.

The last major change that we have made for Max this year is related to food. I'm still so skeptical about special diets and food that I almost don't want to add this to the end of the book. Here goes, though.

In October, Max's teacher came to me and told me that the doctor wanted me to consider making some food changes.

I said, "What are you thinking?"

She said, "The doctor said organic foods."

I rolled my eyes but agreed to try, only because they ask you on your parent intake form: what are you willing to do for your child to be successful?

Of course, what did I write? *Whatever it takes.*

So, organic foods it was. This is way harder than many realize. I failed and failed at doing a complete job at this. I had to go to multiple stores to find substitute of the foods that Max preferred and would eat. Like many children with autism, Max wanted to eat only the same foods for each meal. I would buy a new food and he wouldn't like it. Or there wasn't an organic item in what I was looking for, at the time. Finally, we did find foods he would eat. However, I was rewarded.

After about two weeks, we all noticed a difference. We didn't change anything but Max's food and he started to say short sentences and was suddenly able to pronounce words so that anyone could understand him.

Now, moving into almost two months of trying different organic foods for lunch and snacks, we are continuing to see a difference. We continued with the same therapy and treatment plan, only changing his food choices to organic.

I am not able to provide everything organic, but I do my best to find major food items and favorite foods in organic. I still can't believe it's working. I had previously tried the gluten-free diet and the no-high-fructose sugar diet on my son and didn't see any changes in his speech and behavior.

I can also see a difference in Max's behavior with dyes. When he gets an Icee or red-dye drink, I notice that he can't focus or follow directions. He becomes more active as well.

The "autism diet" is gluten, casein, and soy free (GFCFSF). I have met many parents that have their kids on this diet and swear by it and how it has drastically and totally changed their child's behavior.

It can be really frustrating when so many people are using a diet to help their child improve and you try it and it doesn't work. I don't understand it, but there is something there. How we go about figuring out what it is and determining what foods our kids should or shouldn't eat is something we have to keep testing for ourselves. We are doing our best and working to improve Max's food quality to see more results. The fact that my son is now talking in complete sentences and without prompting is enough for me to keep providing him with organic food choices and one-on-one therapy.

It's important to be clear: it wasn't just the food—it was the therapy first. The pathways and practices were in place. The activities and program gave him the skills and the step-by-step processes. However, it does seem that when we made changes to Max's diet, we eliminated something that was short-circuiting his brain and keeping him from talking.

I really look forward to the future of science and research for children with autism and what we can do naturally to help developmentally delayed children improve before they reach kindergarten age.

Although there isn't one answer in therapy or diet for every child on the spectrum, we have to seek the medical, professional, and educational expertise that each individual needs. When public schools can't provide that support, the McKay Scholarship can significantly improve a student's potential for growth and learning.

At the end of 2017, as Max turned six, he became verbal; within those 12 months, he developed from just verbal to conversational with back and forth question and response. He's gone from being unable to speak to being verbally defiant.

We've also learned that he has apraxia, meaning he is unable to make certain sounds consistently in order

125

to produce clear language. I suspected that he had it years ago. So, now we are receiving specific speech therapy to address that need and help make Max even more independent in his speech and language.

We thought for a period of time that Max might never develop more language, but we never stopped looking for answers, suggestions, therapies, or diets. Most importantly, we have never doubted what our son is capable of and will never give up hope for his future.

FINAL THOUGHTS

This journey has been the missing piece for me.

My son is the missing piece that helps me fit into my entire life.

It's those moments in life when I have been at my lowest and called out to the heavens and universe for what I needed.

The day I found my future roommate walking down the sidewalk at USF who would bring me so much life, fun, and knowledge about autism before I ever knew I would need it. I was calling out that day for a friend who would be kind, fun, and nice. What I got was so much more. All those fun nights with friends, laughing and telling stories, would someday be very important information as I became a mom to a child with autism.

Then there was the second time I called out, this time for a man who would walk beside me and support me for who I was or who I would become. A good man with a good family and a caring heart. I got all of that and more. And before I knew it, he gave me the best gift—my son.

When my son came and all the problems started, I asked why this was my son. I was so defeated and would tell my poor baby that he needed a new mommy because I didn't know what to do with him. I broke down and cried and cried because I wasn't a good enough mom for him. I said it out loud enough to actually hear what I was saying. I wasn't good enough for my son, okay, but I had to do better. I had to learn how to be his mom. I called out a third time, asking for help to be the mom my son deserved and needed.

Through the tears and growth, my son has gotten a stronger and more knowledgeable mother.

Along the journey, I learned about my son and myself. I learned how to fight and why to fight. My son gave me the gift of being the best version of me. I would have never said this would be my journey or my story, but I'm so thankful for the lessons my son taught me before he even turned five years old.

For a kid who doesn't talk, that's pretty powerful.

My life has come full circle. I have changed and grown and life has started to connect on so many deeper levels. That's really why I want to share my story—to give hope, to help others, and to teach advocacy for children with special needs.

I have also developed a marriage with the deepest connections through my son. Through all the pain of marriage in the early years, I always felt that Pierce loved me to his core. When he looks at me or his kids, there is this shine in his eye that you know is connected to his heart. He will never shout "I love you" from the mountaintops, but he does, and he lets it shine from his soul. This man loves his family. We've made a plan for our future and, each week, we keep working on that future for us—our whole family.

I know my story is not one of a kind. In fact, many other mothers all over the country and world have stories about figuring out what to do and finding access to the resources their children need, but I hope that in sharing my story, I can help others.

There are other children and moms who don't have success stories or who can't access necessary treatments and therapies. I want to help those moms and their children. I also want other people to know that they're not alone and they can do it too. They can learn to fight and learn to advocate for education and access for their special needs child.

HELPFUL INFORMATION

Here is a checklist and question guide for parents who have a developmentally delayed child or a child with autism. This is a general outline of questions and suggestions I have found helpful and often use when working with other parents to find solutions.

1. How is your child currently doing in the home and learning/classroom environment?

2. What are your complaints and concerns?

3. Has the teacher, or any other adult, approached you about your child's spectrum behavior?

4. Have you talked to your pediatrician about your concerns?

    A. If he or she thinks you should wait and see, seek another opinion.

    B. Check your insurance benefits: what medical diagnoses do you need to get speech, physical, occupational, and ABA therapy?

5. Do you have an IEP?

6. Do you have a behavior plan?

7. Assess your current situation with your family. What do your immediate family members think?

A. What concerns do they have and how do they see the situation?

    a. This can be difficult or hurtful but having an outside opinion can help move you in the right direction.

8. Make appointments to get outside professional help.

    A. Waitlists can be long, so call multiple places and make appointments at all of them or get on all the waitlists. Then, take the appointment time that comes available first.

    B. TIP: call every day. No, seriously. Call every day and ask for an open appointment from a cancelation. Either the receptionist is going to give you an opening so you will stop calling or she's not ever going to give you an appointment.

9. Be prepared to drive long distances to get appointments and therapy.

    A. You're going to have to take off work and take your child out of school. The appointments will last for hours, so you should have food and electronics as well as chargers to keep devices charged. Be prepared for problem behavior, but don't worry because that's why you're at the appointment. I loved when my son threw a fit at therapy. Then they could see he needed help.

10. Once you have an ASD diagnosis, apply for Medicaid.

    A. If you get denied, keep reapplying and using the term "medically needy child with severe or profound autism."

    B. Once you have a medical diagnosis and full coverage insurance like Medicaid or CMS, get an ABA therapist.

11. Next, look at your educational setting.

    A. Do you want to stay in public school?

    B. Can you get an outside ABA therapist to come to your public school with permission from the principal?

    C. If public school can't meet your child's needs (FAPE), then use the McKay Scholarship to find a private school. Other scholarship options are Gardiner, Step Up for Students, and the AAA Scholarship. Some of these scholarships will let you skip public education.

12. No matter where your child goes to school, observe and visit often.

13. Ask for therapist and school recommendations from other parents with kids with autism for opportunities within your neighborhood.

Autism by Definition

AUTISM SPECTRUM DISORDER (ASD)

According to autismspeaks.org, autism spectrum disorder (ASD) refers to a broad range of conditions characterized by challenges with social skills, repetitive behaviors, speech, and nonverbal communication.

In 2018, the CDC determined that 1 in 59 children is diagnosed with ASD.

What are the signs of autism?

The timing and severity of autism's early signs vary widely. Some infants show hints in their first months. In others, symptoms become obvious as late as age two or three.

Not all children with autism show all the signs. Many children who don't have autism show a few. That's why professional evaluation is crucial.

The following red flags may indicate your child is at risk for an autism spectrum disorder. If your child exhibits any of the following, don't delay in asking your pediatrician or family doctor for an evaluation:

By 6 months

- Few or no big smiles or other warm, joyful, and engaging expressions

- Limited or no eye contact

By 9 months

- Little or no back-and-forth sharing of sounds, smiles, or other facial expressions

By 12 months

- Little or no babbling

- Little or no back-and-forth gestures such as pointing, showing, reaching, or waving

- Little or no response to name

By 16 months

- Very few or no words

By 24 months

- Very few or no meaningful two-word phrases (not including imitating or repeating)

At any age

- Loss of previously acquired speech, babbling, or social skills

- Avoidance of eye contact

- Persistent preference for solitude

- Difficulty understanding other people's feelings

- Delayed language development

- Persistent repetition of words or phrases (echolalia)

- Resistance to minor changes in routine or surroundings

- Restricted interests

- Repetitive behaviors (flapping, rocking, spinning, etc.)

- Unusual and intense reactions to sounds, smells, tastes, textures, lights, or colors

A Sensory Processing Checklist

This is the first symptom checklist that provided a baseline of concerns for us to use when seeking therapy and medical treatment. Our first thought was that our son had SPD because he did have so many of the symptoms on the checklist. We used this information to continue pressing for more evaluations.

Sensory Processing Disorder (SPD)

According to spdstar.org, sensory processing disorder (SPD) is a neurological disorder in which the sensory information that the individual perceives results in abnormal responses.

Symptoms

Infant/Toddler Checklist

_____ My infant/toddler has problems eating.

_____ My infant/toddler refuses to go to anyone but me.

_____ My infant/toddler has trouble falling asleep or staying asleep.

_____ My infant/toddler is extremely irritable when I dress him/her and/or seems to be uncomfortable in clothes.

_____ My infant/toddler rarely plays with toys, especially those requiring dexterity.

_____ My infant/toddler has difficulty shifting focus from one object/activity to another.

_____ My infant/toddler does not notice pain or is slow to respond when hurt.

_____ My infant/toddler resists cuddling, or arches back away from the person holding him.

_____ My infant/toddler cannot calm him/herself by sucking on a pacifier, looking at toys, or listening to my voice.

_____ My infant/toddler has a "floppy" body, bumps into things, and has poor balance.

_____ My infant/toddler does little or no babbling or vocalizing.

_____ My infant/toddler is easily startled.

_____ My infant/toddler is extremely active and is constantly moving his/her body/limbs or running endlessly.

_____ My infant/toddler seems to be delayed in crawling, standing, walking, or running.

Preschool Checklist

_____ My child has difficulty being toilet trained.

_____ My child is overly sensitive to stimulation, overreacts to/does not like touch, noise, smells, etc.

_____ My child is unaware of being touched/bumped unless this is done forcefully.

_____ My child has difficulty learning and/or avoids performing fine-motor tasks such as using crayons and manipulating fasteners on clothing.

_____ My child seems unsure how to move his/her body in space and is clumsy and awkward.

_____ My child has difficulty learning new motor tasks.

_____ My child is in constant motion.

_____ My child gets in everyone else's space and/or touches everything around him.

_____ My child has difficulty making friends (overly aggressive or passive/withdrawn).

____ My child is intense, demanding, or hard to calm and has difficulty with transitions.

____ My child has sudden mood changes and unexpected temper tantrums.

____ My child seems weak, slumps when sitting/standing, and prefers sedentary activities.

____ It is hard to understand my child's speech.

____ My child does not seem to understand verbal instructions.

School-Age Checklist

___ My child is overly sensitive to stimulation and overreacts to or does not like touch, noise, smells, etc.

___ My child is easily distracted in the classroom and is often out of his/her seat or fidgety.

___ My child is easily overwhelmed at the playground, during recess, and in class.

___ My child is slow to perform tasks.

___ My child has difficulty with or avoids fine-motor tasks such as handwriting.

___ My child appears clumsy and stumbles often. He/she slouches in the chair.

___ My child craves roughhousing and tackling/wrestling games.

___ My child is slow to learn new activities.

___ My child is in constant motion.

___ My child has difficulty learning new motor tasks and prefers sedentary activities.

___ My child has difficulty making friends (overly aggressive or passive/ withdrawn).

___ My child 'gets stuck' on tasks and has difficulty changing to another task.

___ My child confuses similar-sounding word and, misinterprets questions or requests.

___ My child has difficulty reading, especially aloud.

___ My child stumbles over words, has speech that lacks fluency, and has hesitant rhythm.

Therapy and Treatment

Applied Behavior Analysis (ABA) therapy is the number one recommended therapy for children and adults with autism. In this resources section there is information on what ABA therapy and what VB_ABA therapy is and how it works.

Children with autism learn differently; with the correct therapy and right therapists children with autism can excel in various learning environments. As a parent, you should read and research ABA therapy because there are different ways ABA therapy is practiced. Be sure to sit in on sessions and develop a positive relationship with your child's therapist.

Applied Behavior Analysis (ABA)

According to autismspeaks.org, applied behavior analysis (ABA) is a therapy based on the science of learning and behavior.

Behavior analysis helps us to understand:

- How behavior works
- How behavior is affected by the environment
- How learning takes place

ABA therapy applies our understanding of how behavior works to real situations. The goal is to increase behaviors that are helpful and decrease behaviors that are harmful or affect learning.

ABA therapy programs can help:

- Increase language and communication skills
- Improve attention, focus, social skills, memory, and academics
- Decrease problem behaviors

The methods of behavior analysis have been used and studied for decades. They have helped many kinds of learners gain different skills such as living healthier lifestyles and learning new languages. Therapists have used ABA to help children with autism and related developmental disorders since the 1960s.

How does ABA therapy work?

Applied behavior analysis involves many techniques for understanding and changing behavior. ABA is a flexible treatment that:

- Can be adapted to meet the needs of each unique person
- Is provided in many different locations, including at home, at school, and in the community
- Teaches skills that are useful in everyday life
- Can involve one-on-one teaching or group instruction

Positive Reinforcement

Positive reinforcement is one of the main strategies used in ABA.

When a behavior is followed by something that is valued (a reward), a person is more likely to repeat that behavior. Over time, this encourages positive behavior change.

First, the therapist identifies a goal behavior. Each time the person uses the behavior or skill successfully, he/she receives a reward. The reward is meaningful to the individual—examples include praise, a toy or book, watching a video, or access to the playground.

Positive rewards encourage the person to continue using the skill. Over time, this leads to meaningful behavior change.

Antecedent, Behavior, Consequence

Understanding antecedents (what happens before a behavior occurs) and consequences (what happens after the behavior) is another important part of any ABA program.

The following three steps—the "**A-B-Cs**"—help us teach and understand behavior:

1. An **antecedent**: this is what occurs right before the target behavior. It can be verbal, such as a command or request. It can also be physical, such a toy or object, or a light, sound, or something else in the environment. An antecedent may come from the environment, from another person, or be internal (such as a thought or feeling).

2. A resulting **behavior**: this is the person's response or lack of response to the antecedent. It can be an action, a verbal response, or something else.

3. A **consequence**: this is what comes directly after the behavior. It can include positive reinforcement of the desired behavior, or no

reaction for incorrect/inappropriate responses.

Looking at **A-B-Cs** helps us understand:

1. Why a behavior may be happening
2. How different consequences could affect whether the behavior is likely to happen again

EXAMPLE:

- **Antecedent:** At the end of the day, the teacher says, "It's time to clean up your toys."

- **Behavior:** The student yells, "No!"

- **Consequence:** The teacher removes the toys and says, "Okay, toys are all done."

How could ABA help the student learn a more appropriate behavior in this situation?

- **Antecedent:** At the end of the day, the teacher says, "It's time to clean up."

- **Behavior:** The student is reminded to ask, "Can I have five more minutes?"

- **Consequence:** The teacher says, "Of course you can have five more minutes!"

With continued practice, the student will be able to replace the inappropriate behavior with one that is more helpful. This is an easier way for the student to get what he/she needs.

What Does an ABA Program Involve?

Good ABA programs for autism are not "one-size-fits-all." ABA should not be viewed as a canned set of drills. Rather, each program is written to meet the needs of the individual learner.

The goal of any ABA program is to help each person work on skills that will help them become more independent and successful in the short term as well as in the future.

Who provides ABA services?

A BCBA provides ABA therapy services. To become a BCBA, the following is needed:

- A master's degree or PhD in psychology or behavior analysis
- National certification
- A state license to practice (in some states)

ABA therapy programs also involve therapists, or registered behavior technicians (RBTs). These therapists are trained and supervised by the BCBA. They work directly with children and adults with autism to practice skills and work toward the individual goals written by the BCBA. You may hear them referred to by a few different names: behavioral therapists, line therapists, behavior tech, etc.

Planning and Ongoing Assessment

A BCBA designs and directly oversees the program. They customize the ABA program to each learner's skills, needs, interests, preferences, and family situation.

The BCBA will start by doing a detailed assessment of each person's skills and preferences. They will use this to write specific treatment goals. Family goals and preferences may be included too.

Treatment goals are written based on the age and ability level of the person with ASD. Goals can include many different skill areas, such as:

- Communication and language
- Social skills
- Self-care (such as showering and toileting)
- Play and leisure
- Motor skills
- Learning and academic skills

The instruction plan breaks down each of these skills into small, concrete steps. The therapist teaches each step one by one, from simple (e.g., imitating single sounds) to more complex (e.g., carrying on a conversation).

The BCBA and therapists measure progress by collecting data in each therapy session. Data helps them monitor the person's progress toward goals on an ongoing basis.

The behavior analyst regularly meets with family members and program staff to review information about progress. They can then plan ahead and adjust teaching plans and goals as needed.

ABA Techniques and Philosophy

Instructors use a variety of ABA procedures. Some are directed by the instructor and others are directed by the person with autism.

Parents, family members, and caregivers receive training so they can support learning and skill practice throughout the day.

The person with autism will have many opportunities to learn and practice skills each day. This can happen in both planned and naturally occurring situations. For instance, someone learning to greet others by saying "hello" may get the chance to practice this skill in the classroom with their teacher (planned) and on the playground at recess (naturally occurring).

The learner receives an abundance of positive reinforcement for demonstrating useful skills and socially appropriate behaviors. The emphasis is on positive social interactions and enjoyable learning.

The learner receives no reinforcement for behaviors that pose harm or prevent learning. ABA is effective for people of all ages. It can be used from early childhood through adulthood.

What is the evidence that ABA works?

ABA is considered an evidence-based best practice treatment by the U.S. Surgeon General and by the American Psychological Association.

"Evidence based" means that ABA has passed scientific tests of its usefulness, quality, and effectiveness. ABA therapy includes many different techniques. All of these techniques focus on antecedents (what happens before a behavior occurs) and on consequences (what happens after the behavior).

More than 20 studies have established that intensive and long-term therapy using ABA principles improves outcomes for many, but not all children with autism. "Intensive" and "long-term" refer to programs that provide 25 to 40 hours a week of therapy for one to three years. These studies show gains in intellectual functioning, language development, daily living skills, and social functioning. Studies with adults, though fewer in number, show similar benefits.

Is ABA covered by insurance?

Sometimes. Many types of private health insurance companies are required to cover ABA services. This depends on what kind of insurance you have, and what state you live in.

All Medicaid plans must cover treatments that are medically necessary for children under the age of 21. If a doctor prescribes ABA and says it is medically necessary for your child, Medicaid must cover the cost.

You can also contact the Autism Response Team if you have difficulty obtaining coverage or need additional help.

Where do I find ABA services?

To get started, follow these steps:

1. Speak with your pediatrician or other medical provider about ABA. They can discuss whether ABA is right for your child. If necessary they can write a prescription for ABA for the purposes of insurance.

2. Check whether your insurance company covers the cost of ABA therapy and what your benefit is.

3. Ask your child's doctor and teachers for recommendations.

4. Call the ABA provider and request an intake evaluation. Make sure you have questions ready.

What questions should I ask?

It's important to find an ABA provider and therapists who are a good fit for your family. The first step is for therapists to establish a good relationship with your child. If your child trusts his/her therapists and enjoys spending time with them, therapy will be more successful.

The following questions can help you evaluate whether a provider will be a good fit for your family. Remember to trust your instincts, as well.

1. How many BCBAs do you have on staff?

2. Are they licensed with the BACB and through the state?

3. How many behavioral therapists do you have?

4. How many therapists will be working with my child?

5. What sort of training do your therapists receive? How often?

6. How much direct supervision do therapists receive from BCBAs weekly?

7. How do you manage safety concerns?

8. What does a typical ABA session look like?

9. Do you offer home-based or clinic-based therapy?

10. How do you determine goals for my child? Do you consider input from parents?

11. How often do you reevaluate goals?

12. How is progress evaluated?

13. How many hours per week can you provide?

14. Do you have a wait-list?

15. What type of insurance do you accept?

For our family we found ABA therapy to be effective. However, when we began treatment with a doctor and therapist who specialized in VB-ABA therapy our son went from nonverbal to verbal within one school year. We are continuing to use this type of ABA therapy. If you do not have access to VB-ABA and you think it may help your child. Check out Mary Barbera's book, website and videos.

What is Verbal Behavior ABA?

According to autismspeaks.org, Verbal Behavior (VB) Verbal Behavior (VB) therapy teaches communication and language. It is based on the principles of Applied Behavior Analysis and the theories of behaviorist B.F. Skinner.

This approach encourages people with autism to learn language by connecting words with their purposes. The student learns that words can help them get desired objects or results.

Verbal Behavior therapy does not focus on words as labels only (cat, car, etc.). Rather, it teaches why we use words and how they are useful in making requests and communicating ideas.

Language is classified into types, called "operants." Each operant has a different function. Verbal Behavior therapy focuses on four word types:

- **Mand:** A request, such as saying "Cookie," to ask for a cookie

- **Tact:** A comment used to share an experience or draw attention, such as "airplane" to point out an airplane

- **Intraverbal:** A word used to respond or answer a question, such as "Where do you go to school?" "Castle Park Elementary"

- **Echoic:** A repeated, or echoed, word, such as "Cookie?" "Cookie!" This is important as imitating will help the student learn.

VB and classic ABA use similar techniques to work with children. VB methods may be combined with an ABA program to work toward communication goals.

How does Verbal Behavior work?

Verbal Behavior therapy begins by teaching mands (requests) as the most basic type of language. For example, the individual with autism learns that saying "cookie" can produce a cookie.

As soon as the student makes a request, the therapist repeats the word and presents the requested item. The therapist then uses the word again in the same context to reinforce the meaning.

The person does not have to say the actual word to receive the desired item. At first, he or she simply needs to make a request by any means (such as pointing). The person learns that communicating produces positive results.

The therapist then helps the student shape communication over time toward saying or signing the actual word.

In a typical session, the teacher asks a series of questions that combine easy and hard requests. This allows the student to be successful more often and reduces frustration. The teacher should vary the situations and instructions in ways that keep the student interested.

Errorless Learning

Verbal Behavior therapy uses a technique called "errorless learning."

Errorless teaching means using immediate and frequent prompts to ensure the student provides the correct response each time. Over time, these prompts are reduced. Eventually the student no longer needs prompting to provide the correct response.

EXAMPLE

Step 1: The therapist holds a cookie in front of the

student and says "cookie" to prompt a response from the child.

Step 2: The therapist holds the cookie and make a "c" sound to prompt the response.

Step 3: The therapist holds the cookie in the child's line of sight and waits for the request with no cue.

The ultimate goal is for the child to say "cookie" when he or she wants a cookie – without any prompting.

What is the intensity of most VB programs?

Most programs involve at least one to three hours of therapy per week. More intensive programs can involve many more hours.

Instructors train parents and other caregivers to use verbal-behavior strategies in their daily life.

Who can benefit from Verbal Behavior therapy?

Verbal Behavior Therapy can help:

- Young children beginning to learn language
- Older students with delayed or disordered language
- Children and adults who sign or use visual supports or other forms of assisted communication

Who provides VB?

A VB-trained therapist may be any of the following:

- Psychologist

- Behavior specialist (BCBA)

- Special education teacher

- Speech and language pathologist

Therapy teaches communication and language. It is based on the principles of Applied Behavior Analysis and the theories of behaviorist B.F. Skinner.

This approach encourages people with autism to learn language by connecting words with their purposes. The student learns that words can help them get desired objects or results.

Verbal Behavior therapy does not focus on words as labels only (cat, car, etc.). Rather, it teaches why we use words and how they are useful in making requests and communicating ideas.

Language is classified into types, called "operants." Each operant has a different function. Verbal Behavior therapy focuses on four word types:

1. Mand: A request, such as saying "Cookie," to ask for a cookie

2. Tact: A comment used to share an experience or draw attention, such as "airplane" to point out an airplane

3. Intraverbal: A word used to respond or answer a question, such as "Where do you go to school?" "Castle Park Elementary"

4. Echoic: A repeated, or echoed, word, such as "Cookie?" "Cookie!" This is important as imitating will help the student learn.

VB and classic ABA use similar techniques to work with children. VB methods may be combined with an ABA program to work toward communication goals.

How does Verbal Behavior work?

Verbal Behavior therapy begins by teaching mands (requests) as the most basic type of language. For example, the individual with autism learns that saying "cookie" can produce a cookie.

As soon as the student makes a request, the therapist repeats the word and presents the requested item. The therapist then uses the word again in the same context to reinforce the meaning.

The person does not have to say the actual word to receive the desired item. At first, he or she simply needs to make a request by any means (such as pointing). The person learns that communicating produces positive results.

The therapist then helps the student shape communication over time toward saying or signing the actual word.

In a typical session, the teacher asks a series of questions that combine easy and hard requests. This allows the student to be successful more often and reduces frustration. The teacher should vary the situations and instructions in ways that keep the student interested.

Best Book Reference for VB-ABA

The Verbal Behavior Approach by Dr. Mary Barbera

COMMON ABBREVIATIONS

ABA=Applied Behavior Analysis – the most recommended type of therapy for children diagnosed with autism and the most difficult for people to access via insurance due to the high cost per hour and number of hours needed in treatment

ABAS-II=Adaptive Behavior Assessment System Second Edition – a form for both teachers and caregivers used to assess and evaluate behavior for developmental pediatricians

ADD= Attention Deficit Disorder

ADHD=Attention deficit with Hyperactive Disorder

ADOS-2=Autism Diagnostic Observation Schedule, Second Edition – used to help developmental pediatricians diagnose children with autism

Apraxia=(of speech) children have motor planning issues that prevent them from making the correct sounds for speech so that others can understand

ASD Unit= classroom with only autistic students, most common in public schools

ASD= Autism Spectrum Disorder

ASRS=Autism Spectrum Rating Scales for Parent and

Teacher – used to help developmental pediatricians diagnose children with autism

BCBA=Board Certified Behavior Analysis – person certified to provide ABA therapy

BDI-2=Battelle Developmental Inventory 2nd Edition – used as a comprehensive developmental assessment for infants and young children

CARD-USF=Center for Autism Related Disorders at University of South Florida – community resources for multiple counties in the west coast of Florida for families with children with autism-related disorders

CMS= Children's Medical Services – provides health insurance to medically needy children whose families qualify

Co-insurance= the percentage that the insurance pays versus what you pay once you meet your deductible

DD=Developmentally Delayed – most common in the early intervention category when qualifying for FDLRS and public school placement

Deductible=amount of money you have to pay out of pocket before your insurance will pay

DSI=Dual Sensory Impairment

DSM-5= Diagnostic and Statistical Manual of Mental Disorders, 5th Edition – used by medical professionals to qualify mental disorders

Due Process=part of the IEP process that allows parents to solve disputes with the school district

Early Steps=part of the Early Learning Coalition that provides services for children under the age of three

ELC=Early Learning Coalition; responsible for running Early Steps and FDLRS

EOB=Explanation of Benefits – provided by insurance companies; will be needed for grants and to verify providers are being paid for therapy; also what you are financially responsible for

EP=Education Plan – used mostly with gifted children

ESE=Exceptional Student Education-the department in each district that will create and manage a student's IEP

ESY=Extended School Year – most people never qualify because the district has strict requirements for proving regression

FAPE=Free Appropriate Public Education – laws that parents should review if they have an IEP and a student in public school

FBA=Functional Behavior Assessment – used after a PBIP (Positive Behavior Intervention Plan) is not effective within the public schools. It outlines what the teacher should do with problem behaviors.

FDLRS=Florida Diagnostic and Learning Resource System; places three-year-olds and up into public schools with IEPs

FDOE=Florida Department of Education

Gardiner Scholarship=the FDOE provides scholarship funds for private education for students ages three and up with specific disabilities

GFCF= Gluten Free Casein Free – the autism diet

GFCFSF=Gluten Free Casein Free Soy Free – autism diet

GOLD=assessment used in prekindergarten to measure the development and learning of students

Great Connections=community resource provided with Great Exploration Children's Museum for once-a- month sensory-friendly play

IDEA=Individuals with Disabilities Education Act – laws that parents should be familiar with when they have a child with a disability

IE= Initial Evaluation – what the FDLRS team will call the appointment when they first assess your three-year-old for developmental concerns and delays and decide if she/he qualifies for an IEP within the public school

IEP= Individualized Education Plan – very important document that outlines your child's goals as well as accommodations and services for their disability

InD=Intellectual Disability – related to low IQ and is a category as an exceptionality on the IEP

LI= Language Impaired

LRE=Least Restrictive Environment – laws that a parent must know when they send their special needs child to public school with an IEP (very important)

Matrix= a scoring rubric used to determine your McKay Scholarship award

McKay Scholarship= FDOE scholarship for any student with an IEP for use in public or private school

Medicaid=Federal Health Insurance for disabled and financially needy persons

OHI=Other Health Impairment- a disability or impairment not provided on the IEP categories

OT=Occupational Therapy- therapy to help people function with skills for daily living or working

PARC=Pinellas Association for Retarded Children – provides community resources for children and adults with disabilities

PBIP=Positive Behavior Intervention Plan – first step in helping a teacher reduce or eliminate a problem behavior

PCSB=Pinellas County School Board

PDD=Pervasive Developmental Disorder-developmental disorder effecting the development or use of functional skills like language, communication, socialization, or motor skills

PDMS-2= Peabody Developmental Motor Scales 2nd Edition – used to evaluate motor skills in an OT assessment

PK or PreK= prekindergarten

PLS-5= Preschool Language Skills, 5th Edition – used in evaluating speech and language

SBHC=School Board Hillsborough County

SDIS-C=Sleep Disorders Inventory for Students, Children's Form

SI=Speech Impaired

SLD=Specific Learning Disabled

SLP=Speech Language Pathologists

SPAP=South Pinellas Autism Project – community advocacy and resources organization in South Pinellas County

SPD=Sensory Processing Disorder

TBI=Traumatic Brain Injury

VB-MAPP=Verbal Behavior Milestones Assessment and Placement Program – used by BCBA to provide ABA therapy

VI=Visually Impaired

IEP Language

Special Education has developed a long list of short acronyms and abbreviations for the educational setting. Use this reference section in preparation for an IEP meeting to make sure that you know what terms the team may be using without explaining them to you. Always go to a meeting with a draft IEP provided by the school ahead of time so that you can do your research. A bad IEP team can use these terms to get what they want and not educate parents on their educational rights.

Accommodation

A different way of doing something that takes into account a person's disability. Accommodations are changes in how a student is taught or tested. They do not change the requirements of a course or the standards the student must meet.

Annual Measurable Goal

A statement in an IEP of what a student needs to learn and should be able to learn within one year.

Alternate Assessment

An assessment that is used for a student with a disability when a standard state or districtwide assessment is not appropriate for that student.

Assessment

A way of collecting information about what a student knows and can do and what a student still needs to learn.

Assistive Technology Device

Equipment that is used to help students with disabilities maintain or increase their ability to function.

Assistive Technology Service

A service that directly helps a child with a disability in the selecting, obtaining, or using an assistive technology device.

Behavior Intervention Plan (BIP)

A plan that helps a student with a disability to decrease his or her problem behaviors.

Community Based Instruction (CBI)

Instruction that takes place in locations in the community and is designed to help students to perform skills such as grocery shopping and using public transportation.

Common Core State Standards

Common Core State Standards in English language arts and mathematics which will impact the way children are taught, how they learn, and how they will be assessed.

Consent

Parents' agreement to let the school take an action that affects their child's education.

Daily Living Skills

Skills in taking care of one's own personal needs as independently as possible. Examples include dressing for work, renting an apartment, and buying a bus pass.

Developmentally Delayed (DD)

Program for children ages birth to six only. A child with a developmental delay is developing more slowly than his or her peers either mentally, emotionally, or physically.

Disability

A condition that makes it hard for a student to learn or do things in the same ways as most other students.

Discontinuation

A decision made at an IEP meeting for a student who is eligible for more than one ESE program but no longer meets eligibility criteria in one of the programs.

Dismissal

A decision made at an IEP meeting to dismiss a student from all ESE services because the student no longer needs those services.

Eligible

Refers to a student who meets the requirements for and is in need of ESE programs and services.

Eligibility Staffing

A meeting at which the parents and a group of school staff members decide if a student is eligible for ESE services. This decision is based on evaluation reports and other information.

Employability Skills

Skills necessary to get and keep a job. These are not technical skills but social and verbal skills that help a person work well with others, communicate with others, follow directions, and be on time.

Exceptional Student Education (ESE)

Name given in Florida to educational programs and services for students with special learning needs (including those who have disabilities and those who are gifted). It is sometimes called special education.

Exceptionality

A disability or special learning need. Giftedness is also an exceptionality.

Florida Standards Assessments (FSA)

The Florida Standards Assessments, which measure student success with the Florida Standards, include assessments in English language arts (grades 3-11), mathematics (grades 3-8), and end-of-course assessments for Algebra 1, geometry, and Algebra 2.

Free Appropriate Public Education (FAPE)

The words used in the federal law (IDEA) to describe the right of a student with a disability to special services that will meet his or her individual learning needs at no cost to his parents.

Functional Behavioral Assessment (FBA)

The process of gathering data about problem behaviors of students with disabilities. The purpose of an FBA is to develop an individualized Behavior Intervention Plan.

Homebound or Hospitalized

An ESE program in Florida. A student in this program must be taught at home or in a hospital for an extended period of time because of a severe illness, injury, or health problem.

Individual Educational Plan (IEP)

A written plan that describes the individual learning needs of a student with disabilities and the ESE services, supports, aids, accommodations, and modifications that will be provided to that student.

Individuals with Disabilities Education Act (IDEA)

The most important United States law regarding the education of students with disabilities.

Least Restrictive Environment (LRE)

The school setting (placement) that allows a child with a disability to be educated to the greatest extent possible with children who do not have disabilities.

Manifestation Determination Review

An IEP meeting at which the team decides if a child's misbehavior is a result of his or her disability.

Mediation

A process in which parents and school personnel try to settle disagreements with the help of an objective person who has been trained to resolve conflicts.

Modification

A change in the requirements of a course or the standards a student must meet. A change in what the student is taught or tested on.

On-the-Job Training (OJT)

Instruction that provides students with realistic work experiences in order to help them acquire and apply knowledge, skills, and attitudes needed to hold a job.

Procedural Safeguards

Rules outlined in IDEA that give parents the rights to participate, receive notice, and give consent.

The procedural safeguards also determine how parents and schools can resolve disputes through mediation, due process, or complaint procedures.

Reevaluation

An evaluation that takes place after a student has already been receiving ESE services.

Reevaluation decisions are made by the IEP team.

Related Services

Special help given to a student with a disability in addition to classroom teaching. Related services help a student benefit from instruction. Examples of related services include special transportation, social work services, physical and OT, and the services of readers for the blind.

Transfer of Rights

The shift of rights from the parent of a student with a disability to the student when the student reaches the "age of majority."

Transition IEP

An IEP meeting for a student age 14 or older. A major purpose of this meeting is to help plan a young person's move into adult life.

REFERENCES

"Applied Behavior Analysis (ABA)." *Autism Speaks*, www.autismspeaks.org/applied-behavior-analysis-aba-0.

"Symptoms Checklist." *Sensory Processing Disorder - STAR Institute*, www.spdstar.org/basic/symptoms-checklist.

"Verbal Behavior Therapy." *Autism Speaks*, www.autismspeaks.org/verbal-behavior-therapy.

"What Is Autism?" *Autism Speaks*, www.autismspeaks.org/what-autism.

ABOUT THE AUTHOR

Ruth Brunson has many years of experience working in public education at the high school level. She became an advocate for special needs children and people with autism after her first child was developmentally delayed and then diagnosed with autism. She writes a blog, Ruthfulness, with tips and information to help other parents navigate the early intervention process. Her book, Ruthfulness, is a personal story about emotional, financial, and educational struggles that led Ruth to understand she wasn't alone and, in fact, helped her find her gift.

Blog: ruthfulness.com
Email: contactruthfulness@gmail.com
Facebook: Ruthfulness
Instagram: ruthfulnessblog
Twitter: Ruthfulnessblog